An Illustrated Guide to the Scottish Economy

The Authors

Jeremy Peat has been Chief Economist at The Royal Bank of Scotland since early 1993. Previously he had been an economic adviser to UK and overseas Governments, acting as Senior Economic Adviser at the Scottish Office from 1985 until he joined the Royal Bank. He is also an Honorary Professor at Heriot Watt University, has close links with the Economics departments at several other Scottish universities, and is a long-standing member of the Council of the Scottish Economic Society.

Stephen Boyle has been Head of Business Economics at The Royal Bank of Scotland since 1996. Before joining the Bank he was a Director of Pieda plc, planning, economics and development consultants.

The Editor

Bill Jamieson is Economics Editor of *The Sunday Telegraph* and has published numerous books and papers including *An Illustrated Guide to the British Economy* (Duckworth, 1998), *The Bogus State of Brigadoon* (Centre for Policy Studies, 1998) *Britain Free to Choose* (Style Publishing, 1998), *The UBS Guide to Emerging Markets* (Bloomsbury, 1997) and *Britain Beyond Europe* (Duckworth, 1994).

A financial and business journalist for 25 years, his work has taken him to developed and emerging economies round the world. He is a member of the Economic Research Council, the David Hume Institute and is a Fellow of the Royal Society of Arts, Manufactures and Commerce.

An Illustrated Guide to the Scottish Economy

Jeremy Peat and Stephen Boyle

Edited by Bill Jamieson

Duckworth

First published in July 1999 by
Gerald Duckworth and Company Ltd
61 Frith Street, London W1V 5TA
Tel: 0171 434 4242
Fax: 0171 434 4420
E-mail: inquiries@duckworth-publishers.co.uk

A catalogue record for this book is available
from the British Library.

The views expressed in this book are those
of the authors and not necessarily
those of The Royal Bank of Scotland plc
nor of Scottish Enterprise.

Typeset by Alan Winney
Cover photograph by John Chadwick
Printed in Great Britain by The Bath Press, Bath

Contents

Acknowledgements

For both of us this was our first attempt at a book. By dint of hard experience we now understand somewhat better how much effort is required from so many people.

First and foremost our thanks go to our four co-authors, Brian Ashcroft, Neil Hood, Gavin McCrone and Peter Wood. The value of this book is much enhanced by their expert input. Next comes Bill Jamieson. From the outset Bill warned us of the perils and strains lying ahead. He also used the experience that he had gained in producing – single-handed – the British Guide, to limit these stress factors.

We are extremely grateful to Scottish Enterprise, our co-sponsors, for their continuing support.

The support that we have received from within the Royal Bank has been tremendous. Jane McDonagh has been a tower of strength as our project manager. She has made sure that we met our tight deadlines and guided us with a light but effective touch. Alan Winney worked wonders – and long hours – setting so professionally the chapters and charts. Others within the Economics and Corporate Affairs teams gave most readily of their expertise and time, as did our proof readers, Eileen McSweeny and Alison Mayes.

Our researchers have been many and splendid. Their work throughout has been endlessly complicated by the paucity but proliferation of Scottish economic statistics. In Scotland you do not just go to the Office of National Statistics and ask for the latest series in the area of interest. You strive to uncover what might exist and where; and then make the best of what can be turned up – making full note of the inevitable limitations and constraints on consistency.

Julie Cunningham, a member of our regular Economics team, has somehow managed to combine her efforts at answering all our (often unreasonable) demands on the book with her day to day responsibilities. Kim White, David Fenton, Ian Hammill, Katie Thomson and Sandra

Langdown have all – at different stages – strived to collect, collate and analyse the multitude of data required for a book of this type. The data base that they have amassed is one extremely valuable by-product of the book's production process. Sharon McDowall and Andrew Wilson have also given us the benefit of their specialist knowledge. We are further extremely grateful to all of those in public and private sectors who so willingly allowed us to raid their data archives.

A major vote of thanks is due to our friends at Duckworth for their encouragement and advice. For a publisher, dealing with first-time authors cannot have been straightforward.

A final word (last but most certainly not least) to Pip and Katie, who have seen even less of us than is normally the case – and even when we have been around have had to put up with us slaving over drafts during the short weekend hours. Their forbearance is much appreciated.

We hope that these efforts of so many are deemed justified by this, the end product. We are delighted that there is now a text on the Scottish economy – to fill the gap that has remained for far too long. But, of course, the responsibility for the book's shortcomings and those errors and omissions which will have inevitably slipped through the net is ours alone.

Jeremy Peat and Stephen Boyle
Edinburgh, Summer 1999

Foreword

The Rt Hon Gordon Brown MP,
Chancellor of the Exchequer

This book helps to provide a better understanding of the Scottish economy as Scotland begins a new chapter in its history.

But what do we mean when we talk about the Scottish economy? This is a question which was raised more than once when I was a student and lecturer at the University of Edinburgh in the 1970s, examining Scotland's social and economic structure and explaining it to a wider public.

First, Scotland has a distinctive history, law, education and political organisation. Much of this has economic implications; we have a well trained and educated work force, and particular excellence in our universities, in medicine and the life sciences, and in electronic engineering. And Scotland has other obvious industrial strengths in electronics, oil and gas, food and drink (including whisky of course), and tourism.

Second, Scotland has been the premier UK location for inward investment. Without it and the incentives of government regional policy, there would be no 'Silicon Glen'. It is less often appreciated that Scotland has a larger concentration of indigenous small firms than other parts of the UK. We need to nurture this area of the economy; that is why, in June 1998, I was happy to announce a New Business Growth Unit and Fund in Scotland, charged with supporting small firms in the high technology field, and with helping to increase the rate of business start up and survival.

Of course, the Scottish economy is not disconnected but part of the global economy, subject to worldwide economic trends. I believe in an outward looking Scotland fully participating in Europe and in the global economy. A Scotland that is internationalist not isolationist, one that does not cut itself off by erecting new barriers, while all around the world barriers are coming down.

In a fast-moving economy where industries, technologies and skills will have to change and adapt our task is to equip people with the skills to move into new jobs and new industries.

So the challenge for the new Scotland is to create a virtuous circle for business development and economic success by linking education, innovation and enterprise.

In the 21st century, Scotland must continue to rediscover its great traditions in innovation and enterprise. Our small business development strategy will assist new entrepreneurs. Human capital more than physical capital will decide where industry is located. 21st century industry will go and grow where the creativity is. So investment in education is critical to economic success.

In Scotland we talk and write of the Scottish democratic intellect. The Scottish dream of educational opportunity for all has been as powerful for our journey as a people as the American dream has been for the American journey.

Modernisation means making a reality for the 21st century of the commitment to education that inspired us in the 19th and 20th centuries – by expanding opportunity and insisting on high standards. So with policies ranging from places for every 3 and 4 year old who needs nursery education to 750,000 students in higher and further education, we will have to build a modern education system.

The Royal Bank of Scotland and Scottish Enterprise are to be congratulated for sponsoring this guide to the Scottish Economy. It will give students and academics, policy makers and industrialists a source of invaluable reference which helps them understand the country in which we live and work.

Gordon Brown

Preface

What *is* the economy in Scotland? How and why does its economic heart beat differently to the rest of the UK? What are the current trends, and the implications for policy?

It is remarkable that the country of Adam Smith does not have a primer that could help provide answers to these questions. It is even more remarkable when a Scottish parliament with tax-varying powers is assuming responsibility for vital areas of public administration. Even more daunting for decision-makers and advisers is the paucity of up to date statistical data on the economy in Scotland.

So, when I first started out to engage support for this project, I had no illusions about the work that had to be done and the commitment it would take. What was needed was an authoritative work that would both serve an educational need in the wider Scottish community and also help put the key features of Scotland's economy on the global map.

I was therefore delighted that The Royal Bank of Scotland and Scottish Enterprise stepped forward with support, encouragement and enthusiasm. Jeremy Peat, the Royal Bank's chief economist, and his colleague Stephen Boyle, have not only brought their own considerable expertise to bear, they have also brought together a distinguished panel of expert contributors. They are acknowledged leaders in their fields, and their contributions will be of value to students and policymakers.

But why an *illustrated* guide? I was particularly keen that this book should have the widest appeal, reaching to the lay reader with clear and succinct text and with bold use of colour charts and graphics to inform and engage. It should never be the business of journalism to take on "the dismal science" of economics. But what it can usefully do is to ensure that economics is neither dull nor dismal in presentation.

The format is modelled on that used in *The Illustrated Guide to the British Economy*, published by Duckworth in 1998 and specifically designed to present key data on Britain's economy by vivid use of colour graphics. It remains, as far as I am aware, the only book on the dismal science to require a pair of sunglasses.

The Illustrated Guide to the Scottish Economy carries a huge amount of information. But there is much that we don't know. Rather than disguise this fact, we have made a candid admission by way of a separate chapter. And I do not mind a bit if this is the most widely read of all. For one positive result of this book would be an improvement in both the volume and quality of statistical data on the Scottish economy. Scotland and its parliament now require it.

Bill Jamieson
Summer 1999

1

Scotland's changing economy
by Jeremy Peat and Stephen Boyle

This book sets out to describe and analyse the past, the present and the potential for the Scottish economy. It is remarkable that as Scotland prepared for a new parliament, no such study was available. However, in setting out on this task, both the complexity of the Scottish economy, and the lack of statistical and analytical data in key areas, soon became evident.

This first chapter addresses some broad questions in order to provide a backcloth for more detailed discussion. It is written with the benefit of the material provided by all contributors to this book.

Chapter 2 provides an overview of the economy in Scotland. Chapters 3 to 10 cover particular aspects and issues. As a conclusion, Chapter 11 assesses what we do not know, due to inadequate data or research.

In his foreword, Gordon Brown, Chancellor of the Exchequer, discusses whether there is such a thing as the Scottish economy. Our inevitable response, being economists, is both yes and no.

On the one hand, the Scottish economy has many more similarities with that of the rest of the UK than differences. On the other, some of the differences are substantial. As shown in Chapter 3, Scotland is an outward looking economy. Global and European performance and prospects matter more here than in most other parts of the UK. However, the domestic economy dominates (see Chapter 6 on Scotland's households) and the prime Scottish export market is the rest of the UK – more important than the rest of the European Union. The links between Scotland and the rest of the UK are far stronger than those with continental Europe.

Scotland is by no means one economy. Different geographical areas have markedly differing economic characteristics and have displayed markedly differing performance over recent years (see Chapter 4 on the regions). As Chapter 8 shows, there are some sectors which matter a great deal in Scotland, but many of these are geographically focused, rather than broadcast across the economy as a whole.

1

A great political experiment is now underway in Scotland – the first Scottish Parliament since the 1707 Act of Union. In Chapter 9 Gavin McCrone examines the complex and controversial topic of the Scottish budgetary position, while in Chapter 10 we assess how the Parliament can be of importance to economic policies and both the macro and micro economy. The full economic impact of a devolved parliament will take many years to be felt, but its potential for micro impact in specific areas will be more readily evident.

Four main questions are now addressed:
• What has changed in the Scottish economy in recent years?
• What is distinct about the Scottish economy?
• What matters most for performance and prospects?
• What lies ahead?

What has changed?

Many of the changes that have taken place mirror those in other developed economies. Thus, the service sector has steadily increased in absolute and relative terms, while manufacturing has fallen back and the primary sector (mainly agriculture, forestry and fishing) has retained but a small share of total activity. There are crucial variations by region, but the general trend is apparent across Scotland.

Some aspects of the broad sectoral trends have been different in Scotland from the UK as a whole. While manufacturing accounts for a declining share of total output, its composition has also shifted dramatically over the past 25 years. Heavy engineering – 'metal bashing' – is largely consigned to economic history. Scottish manufacturing is now dominated by the electronics sector in various forms. Our manufacturing performance in the medium term now largely depends on this sector – both in terms of major investments and the development of a domestic, high value-added, component.

Other manufacturing sub-sectors matter – not least of these is whisky. Another key question is how oil and gas related onshore activities will prosper. This involves both the prospects for the North Sea sector and the extent to which Scottish manufacturing businesses can deploy the skills developed in that arena, and in offshore developments elsewhere in the world.

The growth of the private service sector has been largely dependent upon the financial sector. This sector remains strong in Scotland. But, unless we see diversification and major gains in market share, the days of major employment increases in financial services look to be past.

Business services, on the other hand, are under-represented. There are good arguments that this is, in part, due to the limited number of major public companies with Scottish headquarters. But it can also be seen as one component of a general, relative scarcity of private sector services in Scotland. The trend from manufacturing to services has left us with a higher public sector share of the services cake than in the rest of the UK.

Changes in structure have been accompanied by changes in the relative strength of different geographical areas. The north east and Shetland have clearly gained from the North Sea, while parts of the central belt have gained from the development of 'Silicon Glen'. Glasgow and west central Scotland more generally, have had to adapt to the move away from the aspects of manufacturing in which they specialised. The result has been – after a traumatic period of change – the evolution of a more dynamic and forward-looking regional economy, but one incorporating disadvantaged areas.

Large parts of southern Scotland now face similar changes. The medium-term prospects for major elements of the economy of the Borders and (to a lesser extent) Dumfries and Galloway are problematic. The direction of their transformation remains unclear, but throughout Scotland change will remain the key.

What is distinct?

The Scottish economy has a number of disadvantages to overcome in the years ahead. Location is one. Scotland is both peripheral to the core of continental Europe and distant from the major population centres of the rest of the UK.

Infrastructure links are by no means perfect, and this is likely to remain the case. Scotland's links are made more difficult by distance from key external markets and also by population dispersion.

Businesses with high transport costs are thus unlikely to prosper here, unless there are other strong causes of comparative advantage. There will always be exceptions to this rule. But it is no coincidence that electronics, with low transport costs per unit of value, is the success story in Scotland in recent decades. Perhaps further opportunities will emerge as the 'weightless' economy, built around the Internet, increases in importance.

Yet Scotland's geography also brings advantages. Quality of life is proving increasingly important in determining business location. Scotland, with its rugged beauty and richness of heritage, has major advantages over much of Europe – doubtless a factor in stimulating inward investment over the years.

These factors also help explain the importance of tourism to Scotland. In fact, 'tourism and leisure' as a sector is more dependent upon local Scottish demand than that from incomers. Nevertheless, tourists from the rest of the UK, Europe and the rest of the world bring very significant gains.

The tourism sector has also changed much. Quality of accommodation and attraction has increased dramatically. Now the drive is on to make tourism more of a year long income and employment generator. Increasing tourist numbers in the 'shoulder months' of spring and autumn can yield substantial economic benefits, without the environmental and over-crowding risks of increased numbers in the summer.

Scotland must strive not to lose this environmental advantage. All economies will face complex choices between maximising output and maintaining or even enhancing environmental quality. The trade-offs could be more important and more complex in Scotland than in other countries.

One other area, which merits more attention than has been possible in this book, is the trade-off between output/income maximisation and a more equitable distribution of economic gains. There is ample evidence to demonstrate the growing dispersion that exists between income groups and regions. Further choices have to be faced, related to minimising and managing the trade-off between efficiency and equity.

What matters?

A successful economy has to be competitive, playing to its strengths and generating productivity gains. Management of the macro economy will be largely out of our hands. That is not so much because macro policy is a function reserved to Westminster, Whitehall and Threadneedle Street, or because we expect UK entry to the single currency in due course, but because governments in developed, as much as in developing, country economies are set to experience diminishing discretion in fiscal and monetary policy.

Market forces will increasingly constrain monetary policy – which must largely remain the preserve of the independent central banks. Likewise, managing an exchange rate looks virtually impossible, other than in the short term, and flexibility on the fiscal front will also be limited. Governments will retain the power to set individual tax rates and to determine their own expenditure priorities. They will also have some ability to choose their place on a spectrum from high tax/high spend to low tax/low spend. What they will not be able to do, without facing rapid and painful reaction, will be to run loose fiscal policies, other than when recession looms.

Scotland will be operating in a low inflation, low interest rate, tight fiscal environment for the foreseeable future. This should suit businesses and consumers. The key issue to be resolved is the UK's membership of the single currency, where considerations of sterling/euro exchange rate volatility will be an important factor.

Where flexibility will exist, and hence where scope exists for Scotland to generate the needed productivity gains, is on the supply side of the economy. Fortuitously, policy has been devolved in many relevant areas. We need a boost to investment, in terms of both quality and quantity. In part this means more small firm creation, preferably at the high-tech end, but it also means more small firms becoming medium sized and more medium size firms becoming large.

As we show in Chapter 5, Scotland has almost achieved its rightful share of companies in the FTSE 100, and exceeded it in the FTSE 250, but we struggle to create enough new firms. We should worry less whether companies are inward investors or indigenous and worry more about whether they are efficient, competitive and embedded in our economy – with strong links on the input and output sides so that the multiplier gains from specific developments ripple through the rest of the economy.

We also need better infrastructure, cost-effectively delivered and operated. Continuing enhancement and upgrading will be critical for future economic success. We need to build upon our existing labour force strengths. We have an international reputation for excellence in education which, as Chapter 7 shows, is now less deserved. We compare favourably with the rest of the UK in the proportion of the workforce with high level skills. However, Scotland falls far short of its own targets for lower level, but still vitally important, skills. To regain a reputation for educational excellence, and to secure much needed productivity growth, education and training have to be of priority and managed to suit our economic future.

What matters alongside competitiveness and flexibility is an enhanced *ability* to compete. Herein lies the key to our continuing prosperity.

There is no reason why our trend growth rate cannot steadily rise, permitting an upward shift in our economic performance relative to our international peer group. But nothing will come simply.

What future?

The crystal ball is hazy on specifics but clear on generalities. Into the next millennium a flourishing Scottish economy will be built upon high value-added activities, based upon the latest, preferably 'made in Scotland', technologies and making use of skilled and well-rewarded labour.

Change will be a constant fact of life. Competitive edge will be lost as quickly as it may be gained, unless efficiency is ruthlessly driven forward. Finding the right delivery channels for the right products will be crucial – particularly for a peripheral economy. In some geographical areas the extent of change will be greater than elsewhere, but change looks to be the only road to continuing prosperity.

We will face strong competition within and outwith Europe. The southern periphery of the EMU zone, along with the Republic of Ireland, shows every sign of gaining in a major way from their entry to the single currency. Spain and Portugal will be major competitors for footloose investment seeking to service a broad European market. To compete effectively against these economies we have to be more efficient, with more productive labour, more productive capital and better management.

Being cheaper is not the way forward for Scotland. If we were to attempt a move downmarket we would play into the hands of eastern and central European competitors – and the emerging market economies which will re-emerge as fierce competitors before too many years have passed.

Not all will be change. Scotland's future will in part depend upon making the most of those activities with real prospects on a continuing basis. Electronics is with us for a while yet, not as a bolted on component, but more as an integral and integrated driver. Here again the drive has to be upmarket, with software and hardware R&D undertaken and followed up alongside the major production plants.

The same logic applies to the offshore-related industries and to tourism. In the latter sector a quality product will be critical, as will the safeguarding of what makes Scotland so high on the international tourists' list of 'must visit' locations.

Other parts of services have to change. We need more and better business services. The demand will come if more Scottish medium and large businesses and headquarters materialise. At the same time, business services must enhance their quality and competitiveness of supply. This would help generate demand from those non-Scottish companies that have major elements of their central functions located in Scotland. Financial services developments will be no less dramatic than other sectors. The thriving Scottish sector that now exists will only prosper and advance if it maintains a position ahead of the competition.

Finally, for a successful future, links have to be safeguarded zealously with our key markets. We need full, unfettered and equal access to markets in the rest of the UK and Europe in particular. That access will be best aided by stability in our exchange rate relationships.

As an outward-looking economic entity, Scotland needs the rest of the UK, the rest of Europe and the world. But the successful future Scotland that we foresee will depend even more on our domestic achievements and determination to change, improve and prosper.

2

Scotland in overview

by Jeremy Peat and Stephen Boyle

Output

In economics, as in life, everything is relative. Thus, whether we consider Scotland to be a wealthy country will depend, in large part, upon our yardsticks. Latest firm and official estimates (for 1996 and excluding all offshore oil and gas activity) put Scottish Gross Domestic Product (GDP) at more than £55 billion and GDP per head at close to £11,000. In constant price terms (i.e. after allowing for the impact of inflation) these figures compare very favourably with their 1986 equivalents of £44 billion and £8,600.

If we compare the latest figures with data for 1971, we find that GDP per head in Scotland has increased by 67 per cent, while total GDP has risen by 65 per cent.

Chart 1 shows the latest official estimates for GDP per head for the English regions, Scotland, Wales and Northern Ireland. It can be seen that the Scottish figure is lower than that for the UK as a whole and for England, but higher than for Wales and Northern Ireland. Scottish GDP per head is generally lower than that for the southern English regions, similar to that for the Midlands, but higher than for northern regions.

Over time, the rate of growth of GDP in Scotland has tended to be very closely correlated to that for the UK as a whole. Chart 2 shows the picture since 1971, contrasting Scotland with the rest of the UK (RUK). It appears likely that Scottish GDP declined in only one quarter in the early 1990s. If that is correct, Scotland did not formally suffer a recession, as was very distinctly the case for the UK as a whole.

The oil and gas output from the UK Continental Shelf (UKCS) is treated in the official data as a separate region of the UK. Data are presented below showing how the absolute and relative story on GDP per head would change if some fraction of that offshore activity were to be attributed to Scotland.

GDP per head: how Scots compare

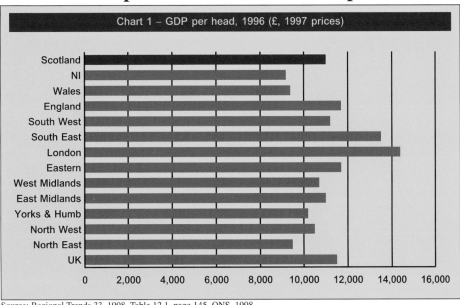

Source: Regional Trends 33, 1998, Table 12.1, page 145, ONS, 1998

Convergent (mostly)

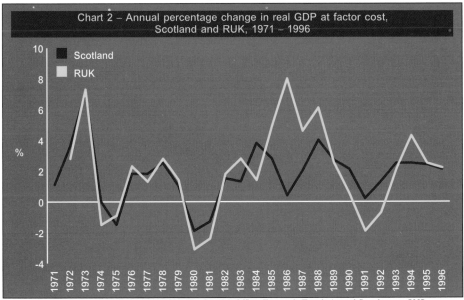

Sources: Scottish Economic Bulletin, 1982-1998, The Scottish Office; Economic Trends Annual Supplement, ONS

On the basis of these official statistics (i.e. excluding all offshore oil and gas activity) Scotland still has a lower per head GDP than RUK. Our figure of £10,800 in 1996 compares with £12,200 in RUK. The average Scot is 13 per cent less 'well-off' than his/her counterpart in RUK.

As Chart 3 shows, a difference of broadly this order has been maintained for many years. In 1971 the difference was 20 per cent – so there has been some relative improvement over the period.

Taking one year with another GDP can be expected, in mature countries like Scotland, to rise by around 2 per cent per year on average. Of course there will be good years and bad years – booms and slumps. Unfortunately, if growth is particularly fast in any one year, then a slower period ahead has to be anticipated. Other than for short bursts, the economy cannot grow any faster than its productive capacity.

This sets a 'trend' growth rate, which it is extremely difficult to raise. The key objectives have to be to keep as close to trend as possible in the short term, whilst endeavouring, in the longer term, to increase that trend rate by expanding the productive base.

The traditional assumption is that, after an economic slowdown, there will be spare capacity to bring back into use. However, if growth continues above trend for too long, then unemployment will fall to levels which result in skill shortages emerging and wages being bid up. This generates a wage/price inflation cycle, requiring government or central bank to tighten policy and slow the economy.

A heated debate is underway among economists as to whether the trend growth rate can be expected to increase significantly in the future. The US is cited as an example of an economy that has continued for many years to grow at a rate much faster than previously treated as the sustainable trend. This has been achieved without any sign of inflation accelerating, despite record low levels of unemployment. This so-called 'new paradigm' opens up the prospect of a faster trend growth rate for other economies, provided that they achieve flexibility in labour and productive processes akin to the US.

How GDP per head has grown

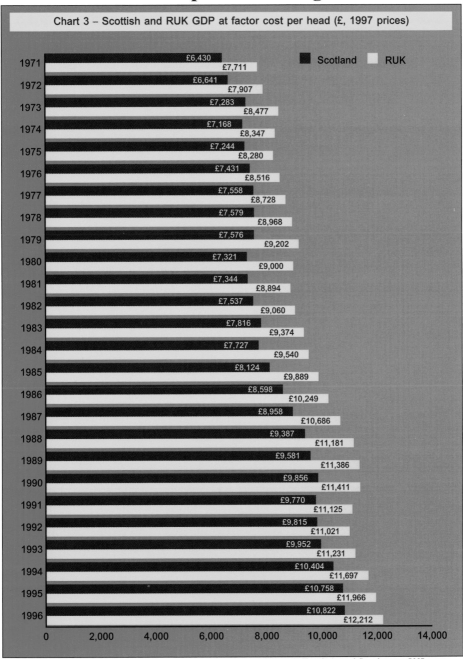

Chart 3 – Scottish and RUK GDP at factor cost per head (£, 1997 prices)

Scotland / RUK

Year	Scotland	RUK
1971	£6,430	£7,711
1972	£6,641	£7,907
1973	£7,283	£8,477
1974	£7,168	£8,347
1975	£7,244	£8,280
1976	£7,431	£8,516
1977	£7,558	£8,728
1978	£7,579	£8,968
1979	£7,576	£9,202
1980	£7,321	£9,000
1981	£7,344	£8,894
1982	£7,537	£9,060
1983	£7,816	£9,374
1984	£7,727	£9,540
1985	£8,124	£9,889
1986	£8,598	£10,249
1987	£8,958	£10,686
1988	£9,387	£11,181
1989	£9,581	£11,386
1990	£9,856	£11,411
1991	£9,770	£11,125
1992	£9,815	£11,021
1993	£9,952	£11,231
1994	£10,404	£11,697
1995	£10,758	£11,966
1996	£10,822	£12,212

Sources: Scottish Economic Bulletin, 1982-1998, The Scottish Office; Economic Trends Annual Supplement, ONS

11

Of course the rest of the UK is but one member of the peer group for the Scottish economy. Chart 4 shows how we compare with a variety of other European countries, North America and Japan.

This shows Scotland in a less than favourable light. Yes we 'beat' Portugal and Spain, but have to concede best to USA, Japan and (just) Canada, and to all the other European economies selected. The difference with the Scandinavian economies is marked. GDP per head in Norway is double that of Scotland and nearly so in the case of Denmark.

How would this picture change if some offshore oil and gas activity is attributed to Scotland? There is no simple answer. For example, what would be an 'appropriate' percentage attribution? It could be anything up to 100 per cent. Purely on a 'what if' basis, Chart 5 shows how the story changes if 80 per cent of the UKCS output is allocated to Scotland and 20 per cent to RUK. Of course overall Scottish GDP rises – for 1996 the increase is from £55.5 billion to £66.6 billion, an increase of 22 per cent. For RUK the increase is much less marked, as a smaller share of UKCS output is added to a much larger economy.

In terms of GDP per head, inclusion of 80 per cent of UKCS output moves Scotland to a level higher than RUK – £12,996 compared to £12,264 in 1996. These results are shown in Chart 5, from which it can be seen that Scotland only moves up one further place in this international pecking order – moving ahead of Canada.

Overall, how the UKCS is treated does make a marked difference in relativities so far as RUK is concerned, but not for the developed world as a whole. Scotland is affluent compared to all estimates of GDP per head at a global level. However, compared to developed world comparators Scotland – as with the rest of the UK – tends to lag, more now than was the case two or three decades back.

How Scotland compares, excluding oil...

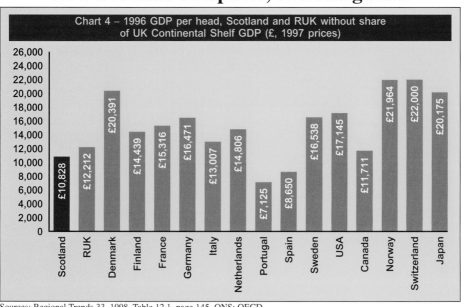

Chart 4 – 1996 GDP per head, Scotland and RUK without share of UK Continental Shelf GDP (£, 1997 prices)

Scotland £10,828; RUK £12,212; Denmark £20,391; Finland £14,439; France £15,316; Germany £16,471; Italy £13,007; Netherlands £14,806; Portugal £7,125; Spain £8,650; Sweden £16,538; USA £17,145; Canada £11,711; Norway £21,964; Switzerland £22,000; Japan £20,175

Sources: Regional Trends 33, 1998, Table 12.1, page 145, ONS; OECD

...and with oil included

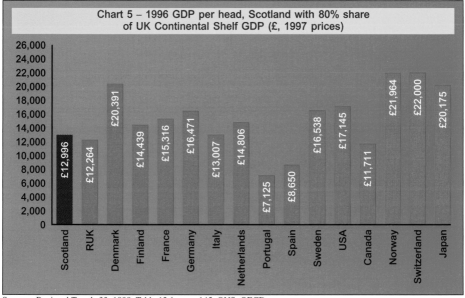

Chart 5 – 1996 GDP per head, Scotland with 80% share of UK Continental Shelf GDP (£, 1997 prices)

Scotland £12,996; RUK £12,264; Denmark £20,391; Finland £14,439; France £15,316; Germany £16,471; Italy £13,007; Netherlands £14,806; Portugal £7,125; Spain £8,650; Sweden £16,538; USA £17,145; Canada £11,711; Norway £21,964; Switzerland £22,000; Japan £20,175

Sources: Regional Trends 33, 1998, Table 12.1, page 145, ONS; OECD

Scottish GDP by sector

What comprises economic activity in Scotland? Chart 6 breaks down GDP by sector, with the UKCS excluded, for both 1986 and 1996.

The first point to note is that the service sectors contribute far more to the GDP total than manufacturing – and dramatically more than the 'primary' sectors such as agriculture. Manufacturing accounts for 22 per cent; other industrial production (gas, electricity and water) 3 per cent; construction 6 per cent; agriculture, forestry and fishing 3 per cent; and mining 2 per cent. All the rest is services! Financial and business services alone make up 20 per cent of Scottish GDP; education, social work and health 15 per cent; and other private and public services – such as hotels and catering, transport, communications and public administration – account for the remaining 31 per cent.

Scotland, like other developed economies, is service sector dominated, and has been for some time. Indeed the comparison with 1986 is more interesting for the similarities rather than the changes. Manufacturing has declined, but only from 23 per cent to 22 per cent. The biggest increase is – predictably – in education, social work and the health service, followed by financial and business services. Note, however, that these increases are only four and two percentage points respectively.

Perhaps of more interest is a broad-brush comparison between Scotland and the UK as a whole. As shown in Chart 7, Scotland may be service sector dominated, but still our economy has a proportionately smaller service sector than the UK (63 per cent of GDP compared to 68 per cent). At the same time manufacturing and the primary sector matter more here. In Scotland, manufacturing (plus construction) accounts for 28.3 per cent of GDP, compared to 25.5 per cent for UK. For the primary sector the equivalent figures are 9 per cent and 6 per cent.

Scotland's economic make-up

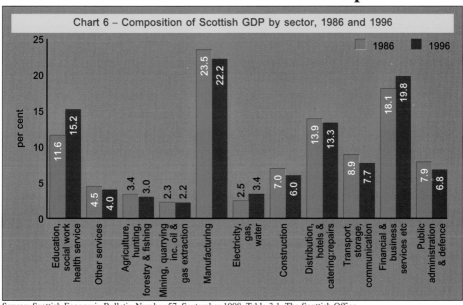

Source: Scottish Economic Bulletin Number 57, September 1998, Table 3.1, The Scottish Office

Sector comparison within the UK

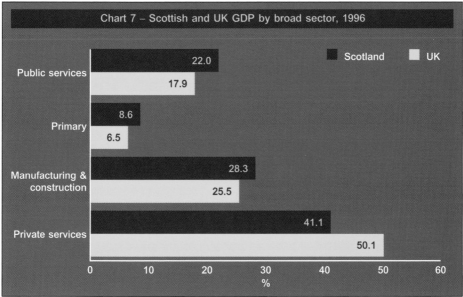

Sources: Scottish Economic Bulletin Number 57, September 1998, Table 3.1, The Scottish Office and Regional Trends 33, 1998, Table 12.4, ONS; RBS authors' estimates

Returning to the international peer group, Chart 8 shows that all these developed economies exhibit the same broad structures – services matter most, followed by manufacturing and then primary – but with some interesting differences. Many of the countries shown have an even higher share of services in their economies than the UK, let alone Scotland. But not all – note the position for Finland and Norway.

Maintaining a relatively large manufacturing base is not necessarily all bad. In Sweden and Germany – which figure high in GDP per head terms as shown in Chart 4 – manufacturing accounts for well over 30 per cent of GDP.

One final point on sectors is that in Scotland the public sector is relatively more important than in the UK as a whole. In 1996, the public sector made up 22 per cent of GDP here and 18 per cent in the UK as a whole (see Chart 7).

Directly comparable figures are not available for all the other comparator countries. Certainly, however, there are concerns that the level of public sector activity in a number of EU member states is unsustainably high, given the continuing drive to low tax regimes and low ratios of public sector deficits to GDP.

Under the 'Convergence Criteria' set out in the Maastricht Treaty, annual government deficit to GDP ratios have to be below 3 per cent, and debt to GDP ratios below 60 per cent, if countries are to qualify to join European Economic and Monetary Union. Although several first wave countries exceeded the 60 per cent figure, the 3 per cent requirement was broadly satisfied. EMU participants are now required to satisfy the terms of the 'Stability and Growth Pact', which requires deficits of less than 3 per cent of GDP, except when countries are in deep recession. Efforts will also continue to reduce debt to GDP ratios towards 60 per cent.

The issue of the Scottish budget is discussed in Chapter 9.

Economic profiles: spot the difference

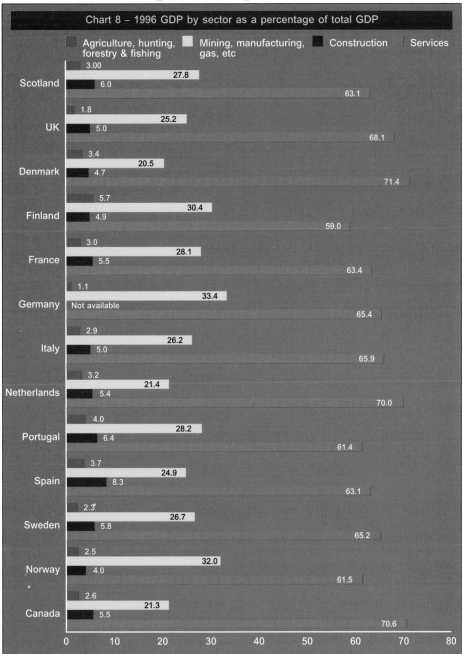

Chart 8 – 1996 GDP by sector as a percentage of total GDP

Sources: Scottish Economic Bulletin, Number 57, September 1998, Table 3.1, The Scottish Office, ONS; OECD

Population

One crucial factor impacting on GDP trends is population. A larger population does not necessarily imply a proportionately higher GDP. It is impossible to be certain what its GDP and GDP per capita would have been if Scotland's population had been higher or lower over the past century or so. However, to get ahead of the story a touch, a substantial proportion of those lost to Scotland in recent decades have been from the more able, better educated and, hence, the more economically valuable end of the spectrum. There is good reason to believe that had such emigrants stayed, GDP and GDP per capita would have been higher. The 'brain drain' has had a greater impact on the Scottish economy than the raw migration numbers might suggest.

As shown in Chart 9, the story of Scottish overall population trends over the past one hundred and forty years is a tale of two parts. In the second half of the 19th century the Scottish population grew steadily and rapidly – from 2.98 million in 1855 to 4.44 million in 1900. This was an increase of 1.46 million or 49 per cent.

This trend was essentially due to medical advances, resulting in marked reductions in infant mortality and generally much enhanced life expectancy. As many developing countries have discovered, in the latter half of the 20th century, it is only after a considerable lag that the influence of these factors on death rates is followed by reductions in the birth rate. There is an inevitable period of very rapid population growth.

So it was in the UK as a whole in the 19th century. However, even at this time the 'natural' increase in the population of Scotland was partially offset by out-migration. This also applied to the rest of the UK. Consequently, Scotland maintained its share of the UK population total, at about 11 per cent.

Counting heads

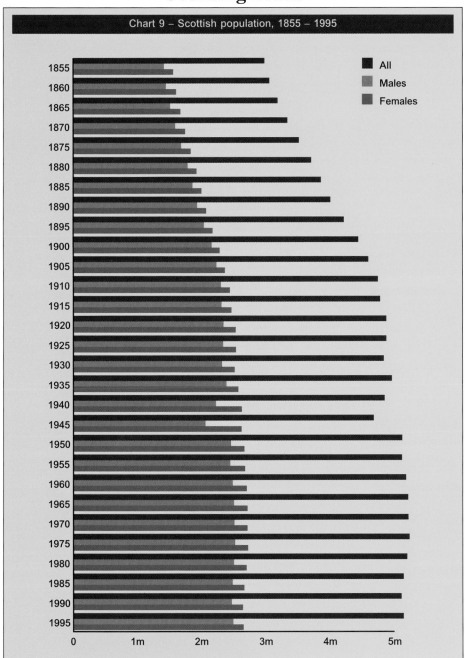

Chart 9 – Scottish population, 1855 – 1995

Source: General Register Office for Scotland, Mid-Year Population Estimates

The deceleration in Scottish population growth coincided with the First World War. The period of most rapid population growth was drawing to its natural conclusion, and the war accentuated the change in trend. There was a population increase of only some 180,000 between 1919 and 1938 – around 0.2 per cent per year.

The Scottish population first reached five million in 1939, but then dropped dramatically during the years of the Second World War, only regaining this level in 1947. During the war Scots men and women serving outwith Scotland were not included in census records. Their return in 1945 and 1946 caused the population total to bounce back to five million in 1947.

Subsequently, population has been remarkably stable at just over five million. The highest level recorded was in 1974 at 5,240,800. The latest estimate for 1997 is 5,122,500 – 2,484,307 men and 2,638,193 women. (Scottish women have outnumbered Scottish men in every year covered in Chart 9.)

Chart 10 shows the scale and durability of the tendency for out-migration from Scotland. For each and every completed decade since 1861 (decades which would be correctly defined as 1861 to 1870 inclusive, etc. but, given the timing of censuses, have to be proxied by 1861 to 1871, etc.) migration has had a negative impact on Scottish population. In each of these ten-year periods, more people have moved out of Scotland than entered. These incomers would have been composed of non-Scots entering plus emigrant Scots returning.

Overall, if net migration had been zero over this period, then the Scottish population would have been some two and a half million – or at least 48 per cent – higher than it was.

The decade with the largest net outflow was the 1920s. However, there were also large net outflows in the 1950s and 1960s, when so many Scots sought new lives in the Antipodes, the US, Canada and even the rest of the UK. It is in these post-war decades that the 'brain drain' is perceived as being at its peak and at its most damaging.

Patterns of exodus

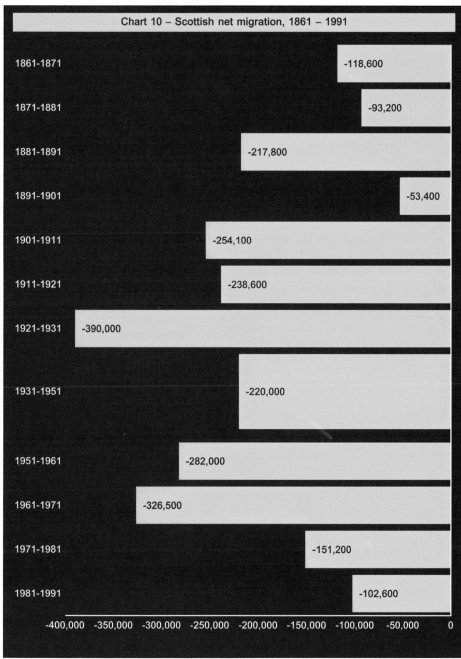

Chart 10 – Scottish net migration, 1861 – 1991

Period	Net migration
1861-1871	-118,600
1871-1881	-93,200
1881-1891	-217,800
1891-1901	-53,400
1901-1911	-254,100
1911-1921	-238,600
1921-1931	-390,000
1931-1951	-220,000
1951-1961	-282,000
1961-1971	-326,500
1971-1981	-151,200
1981-1991	-102,600

Source: General Register Office for Scotland, Mid-Year Population Estimates

Net migration started to slow in the 1970s. By the 1980s migration was causing the population to decline by less than 10,000 per year. Indeed, as shown in Chart 11, it is estimated that in 1989-90 more people entered Scotland than left; and the same applies in each subsequent year in the 1990s for which we have data.

This trend reversal is nothing like as substantial as that achieved by the Irish Republic. However, as in Ireland, it is likely to reflect, in part, the restored fortunes of the domestic economy and enhanced employment prospects. Migration flows are known to be markedly affected by relative economic conditions.

Since the Second World War, by far the main beneficiary of Scottish out-migration has been England. One major cause will have been that in the 1950s and the 1960s the Scottish economy was relatively weak.

Over the past decade and more the Scottish economy has either out-performed that of the rest of the UK, or under-performed less than was the case in the earlier post-war period. As a consequence, the motivation to move – to find a job or a better paid job – has been reduced. This in itself will have reduced outflows. At the same time the costs of living, particularly of housing, increased markedly in the parts of England where jobs were most readily available. This was another key factor in stemming out-migration.

In addition to the factors reducing outward 'push' there were certainly developments which made Scotland a more realistic and attractive location to live and work. Professional jobs became more available as the economy transformed. There were genuine career prospects in the dynamic sectors of the Scottish economy. These acted as a magnet for expatriate Scots living in England and elsewhere, as well as and other footloose souls.

Finally there was the environmental element. In the context of an increasingly cramped and challenging environment, the attractions of Scottish space and grandeur, along with the strong perception of a better quality of life more generally, resulted in an inflow of migrants and returnees. Many of these returned as the retirement years beckoned and opted for rural rather than urban areas – the highlands and the islands.

Comings and goings

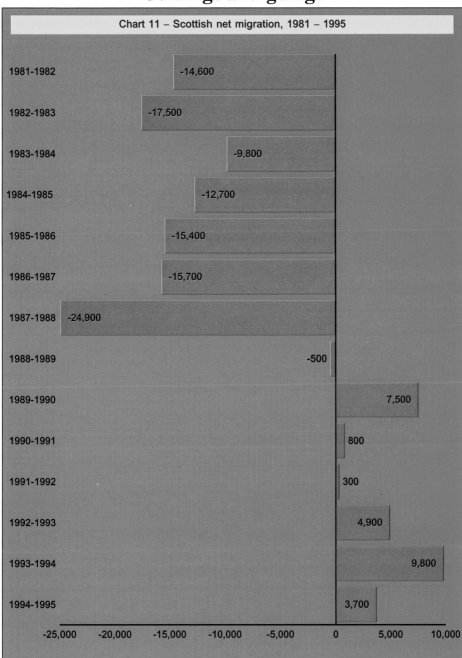

Chart 11 – Scottish net migration, 1981 – 1995

Period	Net migration
1981-1982	-14,600
1982-1983	-17,500
1983-1984	-9,800
1984-1985	-12,700
1985-1986	-15,400
1986-1987	-15,700
1987-1988	-24,900
1988-1989	-500
1989-1990	7,500
1990-1991	800
1991-1992	300
1992-1993	4,900
1993-1994	9,800
1994-1995	3,700

Source: General Register Office for Scotland, Mid-Year Population Estimates

23

Finally, in this rapid overview of historical demographic trends, consider age distribution. As seen in Chart 12, continuing medical advance has led to a steady increase throughout the century, in the numbers of Scots aged 60 and over. This is our contribution to the demographic time-bomb. A higher share of the population beyond retirement age results in increasing costs (medical, pensions, etc.) falling upon the state – without a coincident increase in state revenue, which is dependent upon the fortunes of those within the working population.

As can be seen from the chart, the numbers aged in their 20s and 30s increased in the 1960s and 1970s – the consequence of the 'baby boomer' post-war years. However, the numbers below 20 have declined dramatically since the late 1960s.

Official estimates suggest that the Scottish population will fall steadily from 5.118 million in 1998 to 5.048 million in 2013 – a drop of around 70,000. Remarkably, the decline is concentrated on females, with only some 11,500 fewer males expected to inhabit Scotland in 2013 as compared to 58,000 fewer females. The older age groups are expected to increase their representation, and the younger age groups to continue their decrease.

This is the other element of the demographic troubles ahead. The costs of care will rise just as the numbers of working age, those who contribute most to taxation and government revenue, will decrease.

The problem faced in Scotland is far less severe than in many other European countries, but the implications are equally transparent. It is unlikely that tax revenues will be able to rise sufficiently to permit the state to continue in its role as main provider of medical and other 'caring' services. Tough choices lie ahead, whatever decisions may be taken on the approach to central government funding and public expenditure in Scotland in the new century.

The ageing of Scotland

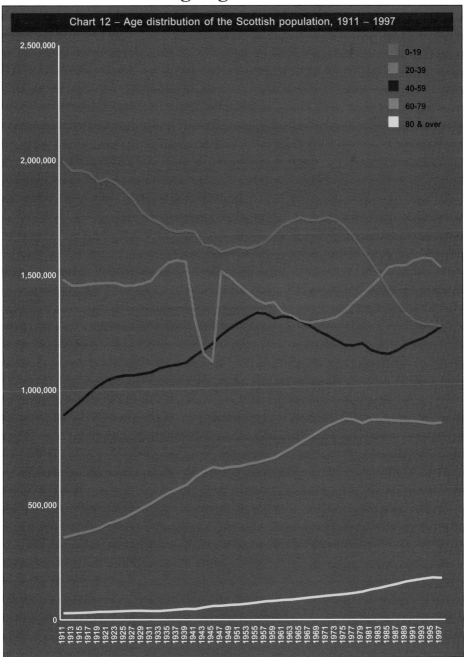

Chart 12 – Age distribution of the Scottish population, 1911 – 1997

Legend: 0-19, 20-39, 40-59, 60-79, 80 & over

Source: General Register Office for Scotland, Mid-Year Population Estimates

Employment and unemployment

As the third and final element of this broad introductory overview of the Scottish economy, consider the labour market – employment and unemployment.

More than 2.3 million people were in employment in Scotland in the Spring of 1998. Total employment was higher than in the 1980s, mainly because of the growth of self-employment. The number of employees rises as the economic cycle passes through favourable times and falls as the economy slows or stagnates, but has remained close to 2.0 million throughout the 1990s.

As interesting as the total numbers employed is how that total is made up – the breakdown between men and women, between part-timers and full-timers and the sectors in which people earn their living.

Chart 13 features employees in employment. The underlying trend has been for the number of male employees to decline and the number of women to rise. In 1981 there were 1.1 million men employed as compared to 870,000 women. Women made up less than 44 per cent of employees. By 1995 there were more women (1.02 million) employees than men (1 million flat). Women now accounted for 50.4 per cent of employees. By 1997 this had risen to 50.9 per cent.

Similar trends to those in Scotland are evident in other parts of the UK. Data for the rest of Great Britain* (i.e. RGB not RUK in this instance) show a total employed workforce oscillating around 22 million. In 1981 women made up 42.5 per cent of that total – slightly less than in Scotland. The women were still marginally outnumbered by the men in RGB by 1995 – accounting for 49.7 per cent of the total.

* 'Rest of Great Britain' (RGB) refers to England and Wales. 'Rest of UK' (RUK) includes Northern Ireland.

Gender at work

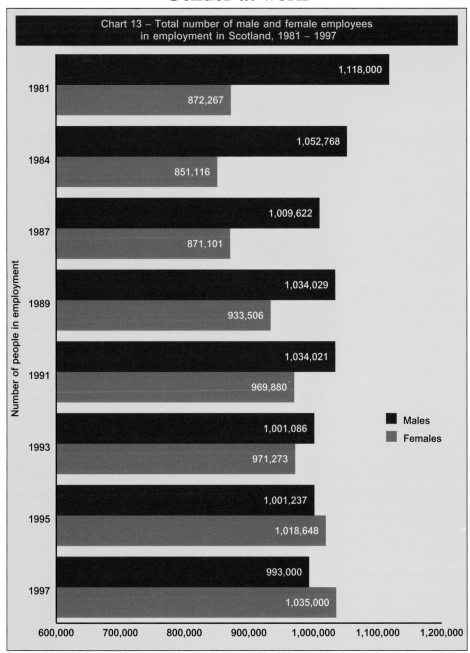

Chart 13 – Total number of male and female employees in employment in Scotland, 1981 – 1997

Year	Males	Females
1981	1,118,000	872,267
1984	1,052,768	851,116
1987	1,009,622	871,101
1989	1,034,029	933,506
1991	1,034,021	969,880
1993	1,001,086	971,273
1995	1,001,237	1,018,648
1997	993,000	1,035,000

Number of people in employment

600,000 700,000 800,000 900,000 1,000,000 1,100,000 1,200,000

Sources: 1981-1995, Census of Employment, data supplied by NOMIS; 1997, Annual Employment Survey, data supplied by NOMIS

There may be more women than men employed in Scotland, but that does not imply that women work more in total or produce more. This is not a sexist comment, simply a reflection of the extent to which a large proportion of the growing numbers of employed women work on a part-time basis. The colour difference in the bars in Chart 14 shows this full-time/part-time split for men and women.

In 1997, 45.5 per cent of women employees were working on a part-time basis, as compared to some 13 per cent of the men. Whilst there are still far fewer part-time male workers, their numbers are also increasing rapidly, having more than doubled between 1981 and 1997. The number of full-time women employees has stayed broadly constant since the early 1980s; the increase has been almost entirely on the part-time front. Again the picture is closely in line with that shown by data for the rest of GB.

One means of allowing for the impact of part-time (and/or seasonal working) is to estimate labour inputs in 'full-time equivalent' (FTE) terms. In theory this should allow for the number of hours worked per week by part-timers as compared to full-timers and adjust accordingly. In practice, of course, the number of hours worked varies widely. Therefore a common practice is to treat each part-time job as equating to one third of a full-time job.

On this basis, the number of male FTE employees in employment in Scotland still significantly exceeds the total number of female FTE employees in employment. In 1997 the figures were 903,000 and 707,700 respectively. However, the trend of reducing male employment alongside increasing female employment still shows through. Male FTEs are down from 1,078,000 in 1981 and 983,000 in 1989, while female FTEs have risen slowly from 647,000 in 1981.

Part-time work: the changing picture

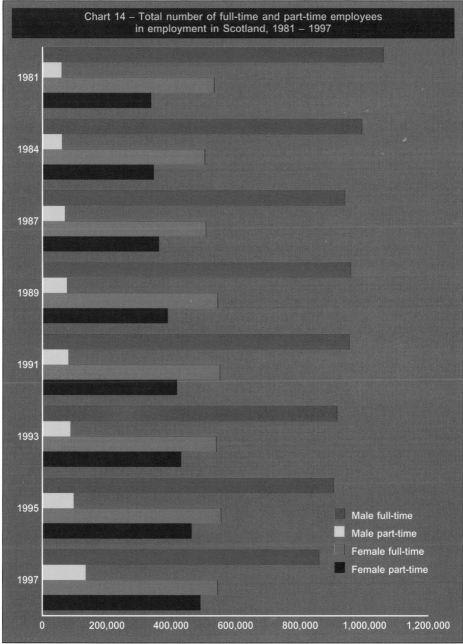

Chart 14 – Total number of full-time and part-time employees in employment in Scotland, 1981 – 1997

Male full-time
Male part-time
Female full-time
Female part-time

Sources: 1981-1995, Census of Employment, data supplied by NOMIS; 1997, Annual Employment Survey, data supplied by NOMIS

So what do all these people do? As would be expected from the discussion of sectoral trends in Gross Domestic Product, there has been an inexorable shift over time, with a reducing emphasis on manufacturing (and the primary sector) and more emphasis on the service sector. Chart 15 shows the trend since 1981.

It is many years now since manufacturing has been Scotland's major employment sector, but at least in 1981 the numbers employed in manufacturing were more than half the numbers employed in services. As early as 1984 this was no longer the case. The latest comparable data – for 1997 – show the numbers employed in manufacturing to be barely 30 per cent of the level of employment in the service sector.

A very similar picture emerges from the data for RGB – and indeed for all developed western-style economies. Employment in the primary sector has steadily declined in this period – from already low levels – in both Scotland and RGB. However, both at the beginning and the end of the decades covered, employment in the primary sector in Scotland was higher as a share of the total than in the case of RGB. Thus, in 1981 the primary sectors' shares of total employment were 5.9 per cent and 4.9 per cent respectively; and in 1995 3.9 per cent and 2.2 per cent. Even the rate of decline of employment in this small, but in some geographical areas still significant, sector has been slower in Scotland.

Part-time female employment is concentrated in the service sectors. Some 37 per cent of employees in distribution, hotels and restaurants are part-time and female. The equivalent figures for public administration, health and education, 'other' services and banking, finance and insurance are 31 per cent, 27 per cent and 25 per cent respectively. The distribution sector is again the area where most part-time male employees can be found, but their share of total employment in the sector is only 10 per cent. Some 16 per cent of employees in agriculture and fishing are part-timers, equally split between males and females.

Where we work

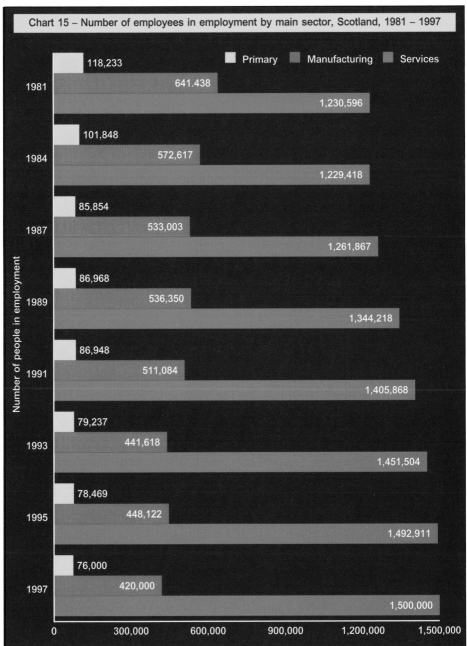

Chart 15 – Number of employees in employment by main sector, Scotland, 1981 – 1997

■ Primary ■ Manufacturing ■ Services

Number of people in employment

1981
118,233
641.438
1,230,596

1984
101,848
572,617
1,229,418

1987
85,854
533,003
1,261,867

1989
86,968
536,350
1,344,218

1991
86,948
511,084
1,405,868

1993
79,237
441,618
1,451,504

1995
78,469
448,122
1,492,911

1997
76,000
420,000
1,500,000

0   300,000   600,000   900,000   1,200,000   1,500,000

Sources: 1981-1995, Census of Employment, data supplied by NOMIS; 1997, Scottish Economic Bulletin, Number 57, September 1998, Table 2.3, page 71.

More finely disaggregated data are shown in Chart 16. Staying with the primary sector, employment in agriculture, forestry and fishing in Scotland fell sharply through the 1980s, but has since recovered. The continuing decline in employment in the primary sector as a whole is due partly to a steady fall in numbers employed in electricity and water supply – efficiency savings no doubt, including those following privatisation in the electricity industry. In 1981 some 44,500 earned a living in the agriculture, forestry and fishing sub-sector. By 1991 this was down to 27,600, but by 1995 up again to over 40,300. There was a similar pick-up in RGB in 1993 – compared to 1991 – but then a major fall once more is shown in the 1995 data.

Attempting to track the main drivers of the rapid growth in service sector employment is made difficult by two statistical problems. First, there are still far fewer regular and reliable data sources for services, being the newly arrived sector on the block, than for agriculture or manufacturing. The data do not extend to the full breakdown of services in the Standard Industrial Classification (SIC). Second, this classification itself was changed relatively recently. Hence figures from the SIC 1992 version are not directly comparable with those based upon SIC 1980. Nevertheless it looks as if the prime sources of growth have been banking/finance and components of the public sector such as education and health. There has been some growth in retail, hotels/catering, transport/communications, etc. but at far lower rates than the two sub-sectors picked out as the main drivers.

As shown in Chart 17, in Scotland female employees outnumber males in all the service sectors. This applies in particular to public administration, education and health, but also to distribution, hotels and restaurants and the financial sector. Manufacturing, construction, transport, energy and water and agriculture remain dominated by male workers. In construction and energy/water, males account for over 80 per cent of employees in employment; and the male share is only slightly lower in agriculture and fishing and transport and communications. The catch-all sector of 'other services' is the one in which employment is most evenly divided between the genders.

Trading places at work

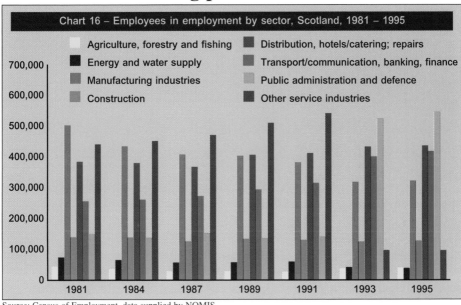

Source: Census of Employment, data supplied by NOMIS

Sex by sector

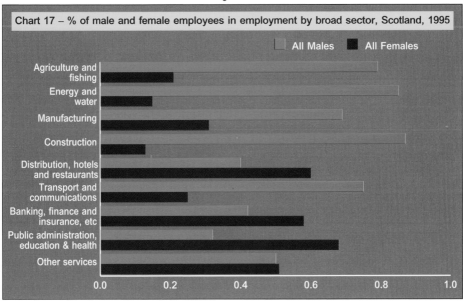

Source: Census of Employment, data supplied by NOMIS

Chapter 2. Scotland in overview

Defining 'employment' is not straightforward (e.g. the informal economy); defining 'unemployment' is even more problematic. Over the past two decades there has been a multiplicity of changes in the basic definition underlying official data. There are also different approaches to measuring numbers unemployed. These caveats should be borne in mind in the rest of the section, which draws on official data.

In general, trends in unemployment tend to be associated with, but to lag behind, trends in economic output. Thus, as output slows unemployment will tend to rise, but that rise will take some time to show through. Likewise, as output accelerates again so unemployment will – after a lag – tend to fall.

Chart 18 shows unemployment rates in Scotland since 1984. As can be seen, the rate of unemployment continued to rise through the mid 1980s, after economic output had started to increase significantly once more following the recession and restructuring in the early part of the decade. Then the rate fell in the late 1980s, reflecting faster output growth, before rising again in the early 1990s, as a consequence of the lower economic growth at the turn of the decade. The unemployment rate then fell steadily from 1993 to 1998.

Clearly the numbers unemployed are also extremely important. In the mid 1980s, when the unemployment rate was very high, numbers unemployed in Scotland ranged around the 350,000 level. Of these, roughly 110,000 were women and the remainder men. Numbers unemployed then fell sharply, right through to 1990, when on average some 202,000 people were unemployed in Scotland, before rising again to a peak of about 250,000 in 1993.

Subsequently, numbers unemployed fell steadily and substantially until 1998, when amid fluctuations there were clear signs of a slight upward trend again being established. At the end of 1998, some 105,500 men and 31,600 women were unemployed in Scotland – still too many but an encouragingly low level compared to the majority of the 1980s.

How unemployment has fallen

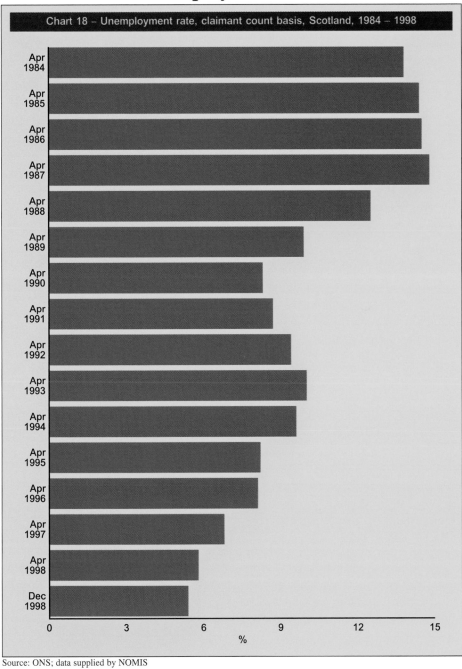

Chart 18 – Unemployment rate, claimant count basis, Scotland, 1984 – 1998

Source: ONS; data supplied by NOMIS

Turning to unemployment rates again (see Chart 19), we see the trend of very high rates in the mid 1980s, followed by decline to 1990, some increase in the early 1990s, and then a marked decline up to 1998. The data for RGB are also shown, and whilst the trends are similar there are differences of substance to draw out.

First, note how much higher the unemployment rate was in Scotland than RGB in the mid 1980s – differences of over four percentage points in both 1987 and 1988. This clearly marks the difficulties faced by the Scottish economy in that period in 'adjusting' to changed times, while the Lawson boom was underway down south.

But next note that this phase was followed by some (relative to RGB) good years. Their unemployment rate rose far faster and further in the early 1990s than did ours. As discussed earlier, the recession of the early 1990s was far more severe south of the border – a case of those that rise furthest having further to fall. Hence, there was a period ranging from February 1992 through to March 1995 when the unemployment rate was no higher in Scotland than in RGB. Various efforts have been made to dig back into early labour market data and it would appear that this is the only period since records began that the unemployment rate in Scotland was lower than that in RGB.

Throughout all the period covered, in Scotland and in RGB, unemployment rates have been far lower for women than for men. Given definitional and other issues, not too much should be read into this finding.

There are many other aspects of unemployment that merit more detailed attention, and a number of these are covered in Chapter 7. Suffice it at this stage to note that, as unemployment has fallen in recent years, there has also been a welcome decline in those suffering the trauma of lengthy periods of unemployment. There have been equally welcome declines in numbers unemployed in different age groups. To many, a high level of unemployment amongst young people is understandably a cause for great concern. Early entry to that first real job, preferably with skills training associated, can be a major plus in lifetime employment achievement. Hence it can only be viewed as very good news that the numbers unemployed in Scotland in the age group 17-24 declined from nearly 129,000 in 1984 to under 39,000 in 1998.

How jobless rates compare

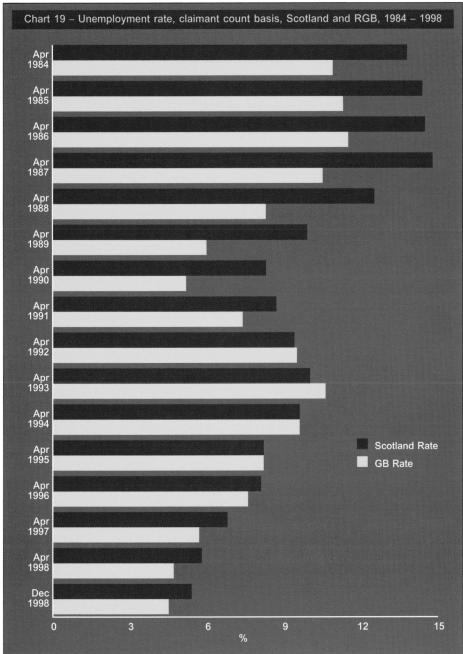

Chart 19 – Unemployment rate, claimant count basis, Scotland and RGB, 1984 – 1998

Scotland Rate
GB Rate

Source: ONS; data supplied by NOMIS

3

Scotland in the world
by Neil Hood

Facing the world

Scotland may be a small economy, but it speaks to the world. Its Gross Domestic Product may account for less than 9 per cent of that of the UK. But it is, as it has historically long been, one of the most open economies in the world. Scotland has needed no lectures from a McKinsey manual on globalisation. Openness to trade and investment has, for more than a century, been one of its defining characteristics.

Global influences deeply affect the pulse and the pace of Scottish business life. These can range through demand for whisky in Japan, the manufacturing costs of personal computers in Singapore, to demand changes signalled by movements in international currencies. Such movements affect not only the export revenues and prospects of giant multinational companies. They also, through changes in tourist behaviour, affect the smallest guesthouse and hotel.

So almost everyone in Scottish business life has to watch the world. Movements in sterling affect the behaviour of competitors as well as the prices of products and sales in overseas markets. And changes in productivity and cost levels also have a critical bearing on the ability to export.

Scottish trade

International trade has long been critical to Scotland's prosperity. Chart 1 shows that more than one-third of final demand in Scotland is export related.

But also evident from the figures is the importance of the rest of the UK to Scottish business. This constitutes by far Scotland's biggest 'export' market. In 1995, total exports from Scotland were £39.8 million. Within this total, £20.7 million was destined for the rest of the UK (52 per cent), and £19.1 million (48 per cent) for the rest of the world. Scotland may be gaining a parliament with significant devolved powers, but its economy has been deeply integrated with the rest of the UK for some 300 years.

Good as Scotland is at exporting, Chart 2 shows that we are even better

How Scotland looks outward

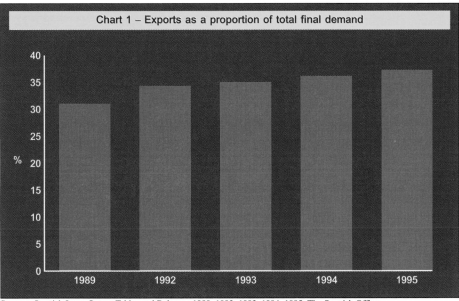

Chart 1 – Exports as a proportion of total final demand

Sources: Scottish Input-Output Tables and Balances 1989, 1992, 1993, 1994, 1995, The Scottish Office;
UK Input-Output Tables and Balances, 1989, 1992, 1993, 1994, 1995, ONS

Big spender on imports

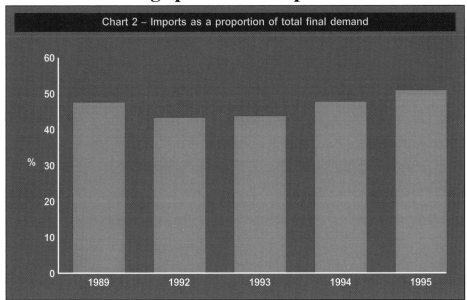

Chart 2 – Imports as a proportion of total final demand

Sources: Scottish Input-Output Tables and Balances, 1989, 1992, 1993, 1994, 1995, The Scottish Office;
UK Input-Output Tables and Balances, 1989, 1992, 1993, 1994, 1995, ONS

at importing – especially from the rest of the UK. Included in these figures are the vast ranges of products on our supermarket shelves, the cars we drive and the components for many of the computers we use. These figures reflect the complexity and interdependence which characterise the modern world.

Taking Charts 1 and 2 together, it is evident that Scotland imports more than it exports.

What does the rest of the world buy from Scotland? About 70 per cent of total Scottish exports are manufactured goods. This category includes the product for which Scotland is universally known and which the rest of the world assumes to be the least manufactured and most natural of all: whisky.

Primary products (such as timber, coal, farm produce) account for a further 23 per cent of exports. The remaining 8 per cent is accounted for by services, including those from the major banks, insurance and investment management companies based in Scotland. Education services are a less well known Scottish export. In 1994 they amounted to some £300 million to the rest of the UK and some £140 million to the rest of the world. On the manufacturing side, exports have grown in real terms from £7.5 billion in 1984 to £17.6 billion in 1997. They have been growing strongly since the mid 1990s, largely due to healthy demand, until recently, from major export customers.

Chart 3 shows how two product areas continue to dominate Scottish manufactured exports: whisky and computers and computer-related products. Together these account for some 40 per cent of manufactured exports. However, the overall share of whisky has fallen over the period, from 20 to 12 per cent. The rapid growth in the office machinery exports (from 25 per cent to approaching 40 per cent of the total) reflects the large number of US, Japanese and European electronic companies located in Scotland and exporting to Europe. This underlines the importance of foreign direct investment to the Scottish economy and the linkages to the world economy.

After the rest of the UK, continental Europe is the single most important market for our manufactured exports. Chart 4 shows that

Scotland's biggest exports

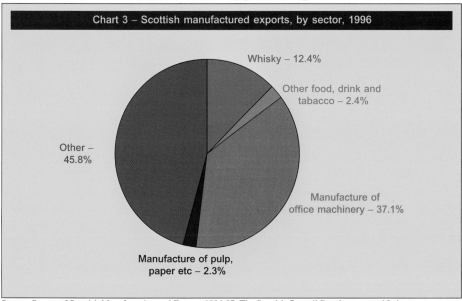

Source: Survey of Scottish Manufacturing and Exports 1996-97, The Scottish Council Development and Industry

Where Scotland's exports go

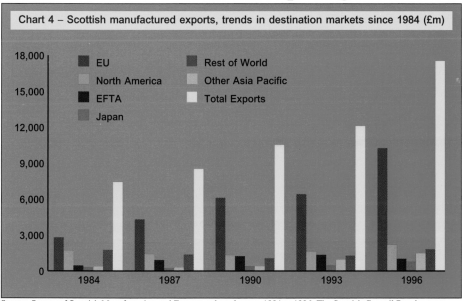

Source: Survey of Scottish Manufacturing and Exports, selected years, 1984 to 1996, The Scottish Council Development and Industry

the EU alone accounts for nearly 60 per cent of non-UK manufactured exports. It is also the fastest growing market, testimony to how economically integrated with the EU Scotland has become. North America is the second most important market for Scottish manufactures but it has a relatively static share. Far East markets are now at least as important as North America for Scottish exports.

How does Scotland compare with other parts of the UK in manufactured exports? Chart 5 suggests that it does well by some measures. Scotland's share of UK manufactured exports is considerably higher than its share of manufacturing employment. This reflects, inter alia, the presence of efficient and technologically advanced manufacturing operations and an electronics sector.

In common with other parts of the UK, manufacturing employment has been suffering a gradual decline, reflecting the need for productivity improvements, and the formidable competitive challenge from developing country economies.

This has brought sweeping changes in management and work practices. It is telling that almost 30 per cent of those employed in manufacturing work for subsidiaries and affiliates of overseas-based multinational companies, many of them American. The presence of these companies in Scotland helps to explain the strength in export performance for most of the 1990s. Exports per manufacturing employee have grown threefold in ten years.

Chart 6 shows Scottish manufacturing export intensity. Scotland has consistently out-performed the UK as a whole for the past 15 years.

Inward investment

Scotland has grown to become an important base for overseas multinational companies seeking to grow their business in European markets. It is tempting to regard inward investment as a recent phenomenon. But Scotland was host to the first foreign manufacturing

Exports and jobs compared

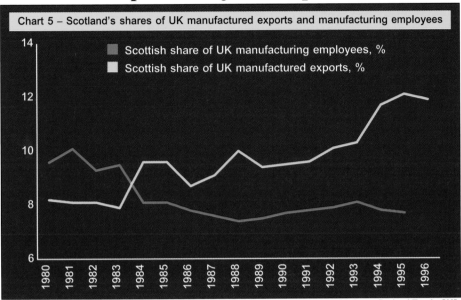

Sources: Survey of Scottish Manufacturing and Exports, The Scottish Council Development and Industry; Regional Trends, ONS

Export intensity compared

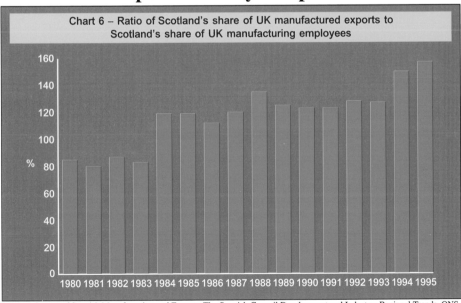

Sources: Survey of Scottish Manufacturing and Exports, The Scottish Council Development and Industry; Regional Trends, ONS

subsidiary of the first truly multinational business: the Singer Company commenced assembling sewing machines in Glasgow in 1867, and at its peak employed some 20,000 people at its site in Clydebank.

Scotland has greatly benefited from inward investment from the United States since the Second World War. In 1945 there were only six US-owned manufacturing units in Scotland. By 1981 there were 178 from the US and 138 from other sources. This period brought many outstanding corporate names to Scotland: Honeywell and Hoover from the US; Hiram Walker and Seagram from Canada; Phillips and CIBA-Geigy from the continent and Nippon Electric Co. and Mitsubishi Electric from Japan. They were attracted by the potential offered by European markets and the lower relative costs of production in Scotland. A good skills base and consistently positive governmental attitudes over the past five decades have also been critical factors.

Scotland was the first part of the UK to plan to attract inward investment in a systematic way. Chart 7 shows the numbers of overseas projects coming into Scotland and the UK in the 1990s. They also confirm that North America remains the single most important foreign investment source. In addition, other parts of the UK are an important source of inward investment to Scotland. Chart 8 shows that Scotland continues to attract a higher share of inward investment than would be expected from its relative share of UK GDP. During the 1990s the Scottish share of foreign inward investment projects coming into the UK has typically averaged between 15 and 20 per cent of the annual total. Bearing in mind that the UK has markedly out-performed the rest of Europe, so Scotland has done even better than the chart suggests.

Overseas multinationals are represented in most industrial sectors in Scotland. They have played a considerable role in changing the industrial structure away from its historic dependence on steel, heavy engineering, coal and shipbuilding. Foreign investing companies are particularly strong in Scotland in sectors such as food and drink, chemicals and petroleum products and in electrical and electronic products. In addition, the oil sector, primarily based in the north east, is dominated by subsidiaries of major international oil and oil-related servicing companies.

Investment from the world over

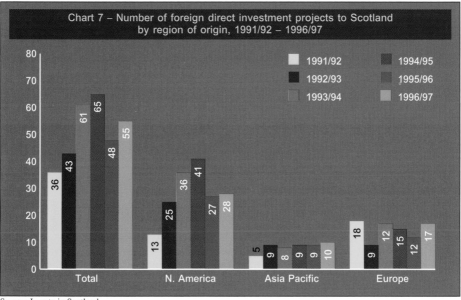

Source: Locate in Scotland

Pulling above our weight

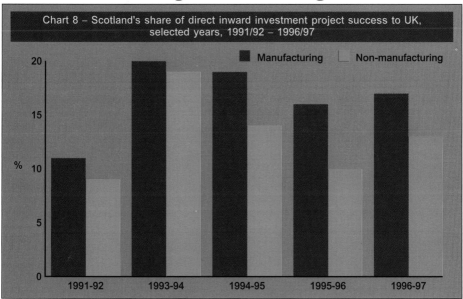

Source: Regional Trends 33, 1998, Table 13.7, page 158

For the past 20 years, electronics has been the single most important industrial sector for manufacturing inward investment in Scotland. Table 1 shows some of the dimensions of this diverse industry. The rapid growth of the market for electronic products, the presence of a critical mass of related electronics companies and the skills base, have proved attractive for electronics firms from many countries.

Many, such as IBM, Motorola, Compaq and Oki, are major contributors to Scottish exports. For example, the Motorola cellular phone plant at Bathgate exports 90 per cent of its production and accounts for some 6 per cent of Scottish exports.

Together, overseas-owned manufacturing companies directly employ 80,000.

But foreign inward investment is not just about electronics. Chart 9 shows the sectoral split of jobs associated with projects coming to Scotland in recent years. While electronics is still in the lead, the growth in software and services is evident. Scotland now has a strong software industry, largely composed of small indigenous companies.

This cluster of business works to attract further foreign investment. The services element in the chart reflects the strength of financial service activities, such as call centres, while in recent years there has also been a growth in chemical-related investment.

Critical mass in electronics

Table 1 – Information industries sector in Scotland, 1997
• Sector dominates Scottish manufacturing output and exports
• Over 200 manufacturers employing 46,000 people (1 in 7 Scottish manufacturing employment); £13bn manufacturing revenues; 80% of product exported to rest of EU and beyond
• Over 400 software and services companies employing a further 15,000 people
• 64% of employment in electronics manufacturing is in multinational enterprise (MNE) subsidiaries (51% in U.S. MNEs alone)
• Scottish information industries produce: — 32% of Europe's branded PCs — 65% of Europe's ATMs — 80% of Europe's Workstations — 51% of Europe's Notebooks
The sector includes 5 of the world's major computer manufacturers and 7 of the world's leading semiconductor companies

Source: Key Facts About Scotland, Scottish Enterprise, February 1999

The jobs foreign firms bring

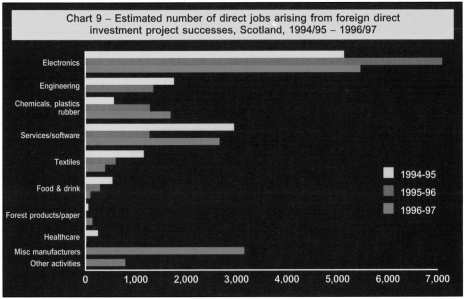

Chart 9 – Estimated number of direct jobs arising from foreign direct investment project successes, Scotland, 1994/95 – 1996/97

Source: Locate in Scotland

Not all parts of Scotland share the benefit of overseas-owned manufacturing. This has often caused controversy between the towns in central Scotland and the rest. Table 2 shows that about 40 per cent of the total of 330 manufacturing units are to be found in Fife, North and South Lanarkshire or West Lothian. In addition to cash incentives from government, overseas investment tends to be drawn to areas where there is an existing cluster of suppliers and related supporting businesses.

The New Towns, such as Glenrothes, East Kilbride and Livingston, with their distinctive environments, new communities and focus on factory building and industrial infrastructure, proved attractive to foreign investors. In the 1980s some 40 per cent of all new inward investment projects coming to Scotland was located in New Towns. They were also the areas with maximum governmental financial assistance and this exerted a positive influence over the choice of industrial location.

Table 2 shows how both the rural areas and Glasgow City have not attracted many new manufacturing investors. But in recent years, both Glasgow and Edinburgh have proved attractive for service industry investors from both the rest of the UK and from overseas. Thus, over time, the balance of new investment location could well be changed. Table 2 also shows the proportions of total manufacturing employment accounted for by these units. Although the average is about 30 per cent, areas such as Inverclyde, South Lanarkshire, Renfrewshire and West Lothian are shown to be highly dependent on overseas-owned manufacturing employment. There are risks here. Relatively small strategic changes within multinational companies can have a big impact on local employment.

Where foreign investors settle

Table 2 – Distribution of overseas-owned manufacturing plants and employment in 1996 by council area (units with 11 or more employees)					
	Manufacturing Units Number	Per cent	Employment in Units Number	Per cent	As % of all manufacturing employment in relevant area
Aberdeen City	14	4	2,950	4	26
Aberdeenshire	9	3	2,250	3	28
Angus	15	4	1,550	2	27
Argyll and Bute	1	0	*	*	*
Clackmannanshire	3	1	*	*	*
Dumfries and Galloway	7	2	900	1	12
Dundee City	14	4	4,700	6	39
East Ayrshire	3	1	*	*	*
East Dunbartonshire	1	0	*	*	*
East Lothian	3	1	*	*	*
East Renfrewshire	—	—	—	—	0
Edinburgh, City of	10	3	4,100	5	23
Falkirk	10	3	2,050	3	20
Fife	37	11	7,450	9	29
Glasgow City	19	6	4,050	5	13
Highland	10	3	1,200	1	22
Inverclyde	9	3	7,000	9	63
Midlothian	4	1	450	1	16
Moray	4	1	50	0	2
North Ayrshire	12	4	3,450	4	30
North Lanarkshire	31	9	5,800	7	30
Orkney Islands	—	—	—	—	0
Perth and Kinross	4	1	450	1	13
Renfrewshire	20	6	6,300	8	45
Scottish Borders	5	2	900	1	10
Shetland Islands	—	—	—	—	0
South Ayrshire	9	3	2,900	4	39
South Lanarkshire	32	10	9,100	11	40
Stirlingshire	3	1	*	*	*
West Dunbartonshire	10	3	2,550	3	38
West Lothian	31	9	8,750	11	53
Western Isles	—	—	—	—	0
Total	330	100	81,750	100	29

Source: Statistical Bulletin No. IND/1997/A3.7, Table 3, The Scottish Office, July 1997

* Figures unavailable for disclosure

How well do foreign firms perform in Scotland? This is an important question for any country seeking to use overseas investment as a catalyst for wider growth. Tables 3 and 4 opposite give us some answers. In terms of total gross output in Scotland, UK-owned companies are substantially larger. But gross output per employee is much higher in the overseas-owned companies.

For 1994 output per employee was 2.3 times greater in total, and six times higher in electrical and optical equipment. As the table shows, the differences are not always so stark, but the principle is clear. In explaining this and the other charts and tables in this section, it should be remembered that these plants are mainly the subsidiaries of multinationals in innovative and high growth industries, whose global markets are often very dynamic. In other words, we would expect them to measure better on these variables.

Table 4 gives another reason for the difference between the overseas and UK-owned companies. The former invest much more in capital per employee, thereby raising their productivity and efficiency levels, often to world standards. In that they have little option, because they are competing in global markets. Thus, the overseas-owned company capital expenditure per employee is on average three times the UK-owned level. In electrical and optical equipment it is seven and a half times larger.

Another way in which the performance of these two sectors can be compared is by looking at gross value added (GVA) per employee. In this case, the sectoral differences are often not as marked. Some of the assembly operations in electronics do not score high in the value they add. However, taken as a whole the GVA per employee in the overseas-owned companies is almost twice that in the UK-owned group.

The jobs… and the output

Table 3 – Gross output per employee, by industry and country of ownership grouping, 1994 (£000s)		
	Overseas-owned	UK-owned
Food, drink, tobacco	191	101
Textiles and clothing	66	39
Leather and leather products	—	71
Pulp, paper, publishing & printing	111	66
Minerals nes; Coke, Petroleum and Nuclear	104	268
Chemicals and man-made fibres	147	95
Rubber and plastic products	73	75
Metal and metal products	125	63
Machinery and equipment nes	103	75
Electrical and optical equipment	301	53
Transport	126	70
Manufacturing nes incl wood and wood products	117	69
TOTAL	184	80

Source: Statistical Bulletin No. IND/1997/A3.7, Table 6, The Scottish Office, July 1997

Spending by overseas firms

Table 4 – Net capital expenditure per employee, by industry and country of ownership grouping, 1994 (£000s)		
	Overseas-owned	UK-owned
Food, drink, tobacco	4.1	3.7
Textiles and clothing	1.3	1.1
Leather and leather products	—	2.7
Pulp, paper, publishing & printing	6.4	2.8
Minerals nes; Coke, Petroleum and Nuclear	2.4	6.5
Chemicals and man-made fibres	6.8	8.9
Rubber and plastic products	4.6	2.7
Metal and metal products	2.8	1.5
Machinery and equipment nes	3.4	1.4
Electrical and optical equipment	13.5	1.8
Transport	1.6	1.4
Manufacturing nes incl wood and wood products	7.5	1.6
TOTAL	7.6	2.6

Source: Statistical Bulletin No. IND/1997/A3.7, Table 8, The Scottish Office, July 1997

One final and important dimension of inward investment is highlighted in Tables 5 and 6. Inward investment attraction is a competitive business. Like all other businesses, the companies attracted are subject to change. Thus, in spite of considerable efforts to raise employment, the numbers employed in overseas-owned manufacturing units in Scotland have remained remarkably stable since the early 1990s. Inward investment is vital to create new jobs but it does not necessarily result in an overall increase in employment: it is like running to stand still.

Table 5 shows some of the reasons for this phenomenon, through a components-of-change analysis for 1986-96. The number of units has scarcely changed. On the gain side, acquisitions of existing UK or overseas-owned companies have been almost as important as openings. On the losses side, plant closures have been the dominant element.

There is no evidence to suggest that foreign companies close plants in Scotland more quickly or more frequently than indigenous businesses. Both are highly dynamic, and substantial changes occur over a decade. Some of the divestments lead to new Scottish businesses owned by the local managers. Others go to new foreign owners.

Table 6 shows how these processes affect employment. Overall employment increased by 17 per cent over the decade. The gain of 12,000 jobs contrasts with a loss of around 87,000 jobs in 'indigenous' manufacturing firms. But it should be noted that openings and closures were broadly similar. The importance of reinvestment and expansion within existing multinational subsidiaries also emerges on the gain side of the equation, and Scottish Enterprise rightly now devotes much attention to this aspect.

Conclusion

We have looked here at the ways in which the Scottish economy is linked to the world – and these links have important policy implications about how well we compete now and in the future. Even more emphasis is being placed on encouraging the internationalisation of indigenous business and the strengthening of links between the multinational sector and local companies. Both are vital as globalisation accelerates and impacts on all types of business in Scotland and elsewhere.

Investment gains and losses

Table 5 – Components of change for overseas-owned manufacturing units in Scotland, 1986 – 1996		
Units in 1986		**338**
Gains		
Openings	79	
Acquisitions from UK	60	
Acquisitions from other overseas nations	19	**158**
Losses		
Closures	109	
Divestments to UK	38	
Divestments to other overseas nations	19	**166**
Units in 1996		**330**

Source: Statistical Bulletin No. IND/1997/A3.7, Table 10, The Scottish Office, July 1997

Job gains and losses

Table 6 – Components of employment change for overseas-owned manufacturing units in Scotland, 1986 – 1996		
Employment in 1986		**69,650**
Gains		
Openings	14,550	
Acquisitions from UK	13,800	
Acquisitions from other overseas nations	3,750	
Increased employment within the nation	11,150	**43,250**
Losses		
Closures	11,900	
Divestments to UK	6,700	
Divestments to other overseas nations	4,700	
Decreased employment within the nation	7,850	**31,150**
Employment in 1996		**81,750**

Source: Statistical Bulletin No. IND/1997/A3.7, Table 11, The Scottish Office, July 1997

4

The regions

by Jeremy Peat and Stephen Boyle

Scotland and the regions

Scotland is by no means just one economy, but a large cluster of 'micro' regions. The central belt contains the majority of the population and accounts for the bulk of economic output. However, its economy is very different from that of the borders, the highlands, the islands (the Western Isles, Orkney and Shetland all exhibit marked differences between each other) and the oil-affected north east.

In this chapter we generally use the classification of the Scottish regions in existence before the 1996 local government re-organisation. This is a pragmatic choice, as most data exist at this level. It also permits a manageable discussion, which can take account of the key economic differences. In some instances more recent data for the new Scottish local authority areas are also discussed.

Population

Charts 1 and 2 show the breakdown of population within Scotland, both in 1997 and for comparison in 1971.

The dominance of Strathclyde is stark, but declining – from 49.2 per cent in 1971 to 44.4 per cent in 1997. Lothian, Grampian, Tayside, Fife and Central come next in scale – in that order. All of these regions increased their share of Scotland's population over the period. For Grampian the increase was substantial – a rise of more than 86,000 to 528,400, reflecting the impact of oil and gas. Highland's share also rose sharply, from 3.3 per cent to 4.1 per cent.

The two southern regions each account for between 2 and 3 per cent of the total with both absolute population increases and increased shares of the total. Taken together the Western Isles, Orkney and Shetland account for less than 1.5 per cent of the total, but with some increase of late in the northern isles, particularly Shetland – again due to oil. The Western Isles is the only region, along with the big loser Strathclyde, to have suffered a reduction in population share over the period.

Where we lived then...

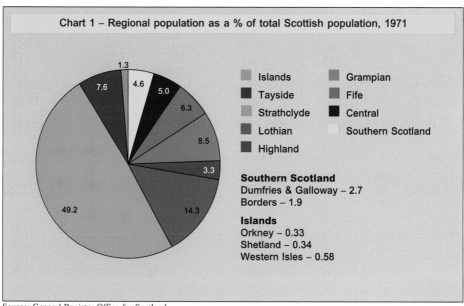

Chart 1 – Regional population as a % of total Scottish population, 1971

Islands   Grampian
Tayside   Fife
Strathclyde   Central
Lothian   Southern Scotland
Highland

Southern Scotland
Dumfries & Galloway – 2.7
Borders – 1.9
Islands
Orkney – 0.33
Shetland – 0.34
Western Isles – 0.58

Source: General Register Office for Scotland

...and where now

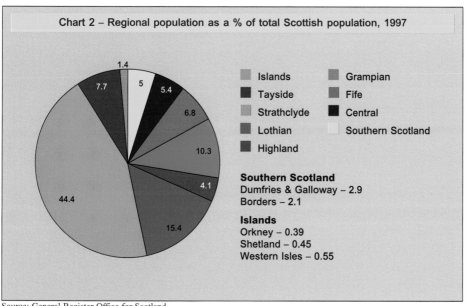

Chart 2 – Regional population as a % of total Scottish population, 1997

Islands   Grampian
Tayside   Fife
Strathclyde   Central
Lothian   Southern Scotland
Highland

Southern Scotland
Dumfries & Galloway – 2.9
Borders – 2.1
Islands
Orkney – 0.39
Shetland – 0.45
Western Isles – 0.55

Source: General Register Office for Scotland

Gross Domestic Product

There is also a significant variation in relative affluence between the regions. As shown in Chart 4, Grampian had (in 1995) the highest Gross Domestic Product per head, followed by Lothian. At the other end of the scale the Highlands and Islands (combined, separate data are not available) and Strathclyde show the lowest GDP per head. Borders, Central, Strathclyde, Tayside and Dumfries and Galloway (in that order) came next, all still below the Scotland average.

Chart 3 shows the equivalent figures for 1977 (data are not available for Borders). Comparison of the two charts shows both that there have been changes in the affluence rankings and that the variation between regions has become much more marked over time. In 1977 GDP per head was again highest in Grampian, but at this time followed in a tight grouping by Central, Fife, Highlands and Islands and then Lothian. These regions were all just above the Scotland average level, with (in ascending order) Strathclyde, Tayside and Dumfries and Galloway only marginally below that level.

In 1977 the gap between richest and poorest region was 18 per cent. By 1995 it had leapt to 62 per cent.

Data for 1996 are available for the new local authority areas. GDP per head is highest in Edinburgh, nearly £1,500 higher than in north eastern Scotland – a combination of Aberdeen City, Aberdeenshire and North East Moray. Next in line come West Lothian, Glasgow City and Shetland Islands. The lowest figure cited is for the combination of East Lothian and Midlothian – at £6,116 compared to £16,199 in neighbouring Edinburgh City. A number of other areas in the central belt as well as the Highlands and Western Isles have GDP per head between £7,000 and £9,000.

Scotland's wealth in 1977...

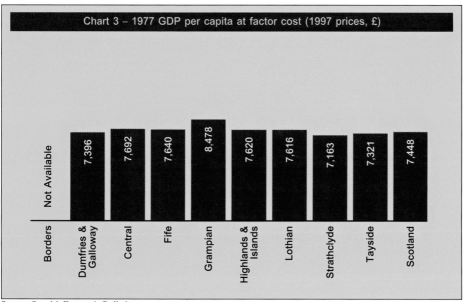

Source: Scottish Economic Bulletin

...and the picture now

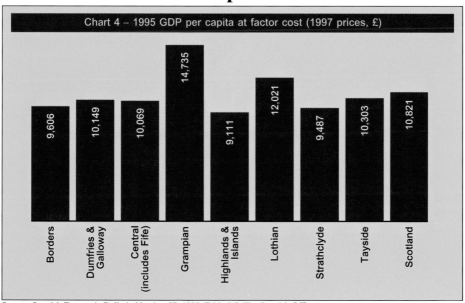

Source: Scottish Economic Bulletin Number 57, 1998, Table 9.5, The Scottish Office

Average earnings

GDP per head can vary between geographical areas for a variety of reasons. One key factor is variation in average earnings. Chart 5 sets out average earnings by region, for 1996, for all full-time workers. The Scotland and GB figures are also shown, by way of comparison.

Overall average earnings per head are highest in Grampian, the only Scottish region where earnings per head in 1996 were greater than the GB average, followed by Lothian. Overall average earnings per head are lowest in Dumfries and Galloway and Highland region, but also well below the Scottish average in Borders and Fife.

Chart 6 shows data for males and females – but with gaps for some regions due to sample limitations. For males, earnings are highest for Grampian, again above the GB average. Next come Central and Lothian. Male average earnings are lowest in Dumfries and Galloway and the Highlands.

For females, the pattern is slightly different. In all regions female average earnings are below the GB average. Female earnings are highest in Lothian. Female earnings in Grampian are broadly on a par with those in Strathclyde and Scotland as a whole.

Data are available for 1998, for most of the new Scottish local authority areas. Again, there are gaps due to data constraints. These show male earnings to be far higher in Aberdeen City than elsewhere, followed by Edinburgh, Aberdeenshire and Glasgow. A very low figure for East Lothian again shows the wide variation within the old Lothian region.

According to these data, Edinburgh, Dundee and Glasgow all show higher female average earnings than Aberdeen. Female average earnings are relatively low in Aberdeenshire and Highland.

How pay varies by region

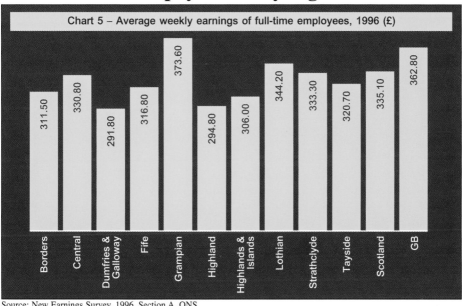

Chart 5 – Average weekly earnings of full-time employees, 1996 (£)

Region	Earnings (£)
Borders	311.50
Central	330.80
Dumfries & Galloway	291.80
Fife	316.80
Grampian	373.60
Highland	294.80
Highlands & Islands	306.00
Lothian	344.20
Strathclyde	333.30
Tayside	320.70
Scotland	335.10
GB	362.80

Source: New Earnings Survey, 1996, Section A, ONS

Male earners still lead

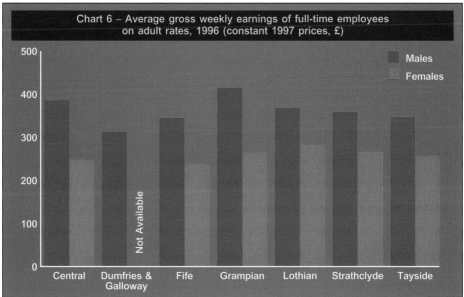

Chart 6 – Average gross weekly earnings of full-time employees on adult rates, 1996 (constant 1997 prices, £)

Males
Females

Central, Dumfries & Galloway (Not Available), Fife, Grampian, Lothian, Strathclyde, Tayside

Source: New Earnings Survey, 1996, Part E, Table 110, ONS

Sectoral structure

As is clear from Chapter 2, the Scottish economy is dominated by the service sector, with manufacturing accounting for a declining share of employment and output and the primary sector of only limited significance.

This is also broadly true for each of Scotland's regions. Of course, agriculture is relatively more important to the Borders economy than it is to Strathclyde. But showing a straight sectoral breakdown by region would not be immensely revealing.

Therefore, Table 1 shows the differences in sectoral employment, based upon the extent of variation from the Scottish norm. For each region the percentage share of employment by sector is contrasted with that for Scotland, to show whether that sector is more or less important, in employment terms, in that region, as compared with Scotland as a whole. Arithmetically, the percentage share for the region is divided by the percentage share for Scotland. If the 'quotient' derived is greater than unity, then that sector matters more in the region concerned than is the norm for Scotland. If the 'quotient' is less than one, then the sector is under-represented.

A simple example may aid understanding. In the Borders, agriculture, forestry and fishing accounted for 6.7 per cent of total employment in 1996, compared with 1.7 per cent for Scotland as a whole. The Borders quotient for that sector is 4.0 (6.7 divided by 1.7). In other words, something like four times as many people are employed in this sector in the Borders than would be the case if the employment structure there were identical to the Scottish average.

The Borders shows over-representation in agriculture, etc and manufacturing and under-representation in all private services, while **Central Region** is closer to the Scottish norm – somewhat over-represented in manufacturing and under-represented in the primary sector.

Dumfries and Galloway is similar to Borders, with agriculture, etc, heavily over-represented and manufacturing less so. But it is holding its own in distribution, hotels and restaurants, albeit under-represented in financial and business services, public administration and 'other' services.

Fife is over-represented in manufacturing, and under-represented in agriculture, etc, construction, banking/finance and transport/ communications.

Grampian is dramatically above the norm in energy and water, also somewhat above average for construction and agriculture, etc.

The Highland Region is, like the southern regions, heavily above average in agriculture, etc, but also above the norm for construction and distribution and hotels and under-represented in manufacturing and energy/water.

In **Lothian,** employment in banking, finance, insurance is well above average and all non-service sectors markedly under-represented.

Strathclyde Region is under-represented in the primary sectors, otherwise broadly in line with Scotland as a whole – unsurprisingly given that it accounts for 44 per cent of the total population.

Employment in **Tayside** is above average for agriculture, etc and below average for banking/finance/insurance, transport and construction.

In both **Orkney and Shetland Islands** agriculture, etc, energy/water and transport/communications are heavily over-represented while manufacturing and banking/finance fall well short of the average employment shares.

As with the northern isles, in the **Western Isles** agriculture, etc, is relatively over-represented and manufacturing and banking/finance under the norm; but energy/water is a weakness – no North Sea oil impact here as there has been in the northern isles.

The way we work

Table 1 – Regional location quotients, Scotland, 1996			
Region	Quotient	Region	Quotient
Borders		**Fife**	
Agriculture, etc	4.0	Agriculture, etc	0.8
Energy and water	0.3	Energy and water	1.0
Manufacturing	1.7	Manufacturing	1.4
Construction	0.9	Construction	0.7
Distribution, hotels & restaurants	0.9	Distribution, hotels & restaurants	1.0
Transport and communications	0.4	Transport and communications	0.7
Banking, finance and insurance, etc	0.5	Banking, finance and insurance, etc	0.6
Public administration, education & health	1.0	Public administration, education & health	1.1
Other services	0.6	Other services	1.1
Central		**Grampian**	
Agriculture, etc	0.8	Agriculture, etc	1.3
Energy and water	0.7	Energy and water	3.4
Manufacturing	1.2	Manufacturing	0.8
Construction	1.0	Construction	1.5
Distribution, hotels & restaurants	1.1	Distribution, hotels & restaurants	0.9
Transport and communications	0.9	Transport and communications	1.0
Banking, finance and insurance, etc	0.7	Banking, finance and insurance, etc	1.1
Public administration, education & health	1.0	Public administration, education & health	0.8
Other services	0.9	Other services	1.1
Dumfries & Galloway		**Highland**	
Agriculture, etc	4.8	Agriculture, etc	2.6
Energy and water	1.0	Energy and water	0.6
Manufacturing	1.2	Manufacturing	0.7
Construction	1.0	Construction	1.2
Distribution, hotels & restaurants	1.1	Distribution, hotels & restaurants	1.2
Transport and communications	1.2	Transport and communications	1.0
Banking, finance and insurance, etc	0.5	Banking, finance and insurance, etc	1.0
Public administration, education & health	0.8	Public administration, education & health	1.0
Other services	0.9	Other services	0.9

For the purpose of calculating quotients, Scotland is the 'base' area.

Table 1 – Regional location quotients, Scotland, 1996			
Region	Quotient	Region	Quotient
Lothian		**Strathclyde**	
Agriculture, etc	0.5	Agriculture, etc	0.5
Energy and water	0.5	Energy and water	0.6
Manufacturing	0.8	Manufacturing	1.1
Construction	0.7	Construction	1.0
Distribution, hotels & restaurants	0.9	Distribution, hotels & restaurants	1.0
Transport and communications	0.9	Transport and communications	1.1
Banking, finance and insurance, etc	1.4	Banking, finance and insurance, etc	1.0
Public administration, education & health	1.1	Public administration, education & health	1.0
Other services	1.0	Other services	1.0
Orkney Islands		**Tayside**	
Agriculture, etc	4.5	Agriculture, etc	1.4
Energy and water	1.7	Energy and water	0.7
Manufacturing	0.6	Manufacturing	1.0
Construction	1.4	Construction	0.9
Distribution, hotels & restaurants	1.0	Distribution, hotels & restaurants	1.2
Transport and communications	1.9	Transport and communications	0.9
Banking, finance and insurance, etc	0.3	Banking, finance and insurance, etc	0.7
Public administration, education & health	1.2	Public administration, education & health	1.0
Other services	0.7	Other services	1.0
Shetland Islands		**Western Isles**	
Agriculture, etc	4.4	Agriculture, etc	3.8
Energy and water	2.9	Energy and water	0.5
Manufacturing	0.5	Manufacturing	0.6
Construction	1.2	Construction	1.4
Distribution, hotels & restaurants	0.9	Distribution, hotels & restaurants	1.0
Transport and communications	2.1	Transport and communications	1.0
Banking, finance and insurance, etc	0.4	Banking, finance and insurance, etc	0.4
Public administration, education & health	1.1	Public administration, education & health	1.4
Other services	1.1	Other services	0.5

Source: Derived from Annual Employment Survey, data supplied by NOMIS

Unemployment

These variations in employment structure help to explain regional differences in relative affluence and in unemployment rates. Charts 7 and 7a show how regional unemployment rates have varied since 1984. The data used are for April of each year, and then end 1998. In some regions there are significant variations in employment rates through the year, due to seasonally related activities such as tourism. The data for April should be reasonably 'neutral' so far as seasonality is concerned.

Unemployment has tended to fall significantly over the past 14 or 15 years, falling steadily until the early 1990s, then rising until around 1993 or 1994, before declining once more and then stabilising in 1998. However, broadly the same cyclical movements can be seen to apply across the regions, and the rankings by unemployment rate do not alter dramatically over the period.

In April 1984 the regions with the lowest unemployment rates (in ascending order) were Grampian, the Shetlands, Borders and the Orkneys. Those same four regions maintained their (relative) low unemployment status right through to April 1998. Over the past couple of years the unemployment rate in the Lothians has fallen particularly fast, bringing that region into contention. Unemployment in Grampian can be seen (particularly from the detailed data) to exhibit something of a different trend, as a consequence of the influence of the oil cycle and oil-related activities.

At the other end of the spectrum, in April 1984 the highest regional unemployment rate was in Strathclyde – at 17.1 per cent. Next highest were the Western Isles and Central Region. Unemployment continues to affect the Western Isles markedly, which had the highest regional unemployment rate at the end of 1998, despite having fallen from 15.5 per cent in 1984 to 8.7 per cent in December 1998. Next, in descending order, came Strathclyde, Fife, Central, Tayside, Dumfries and Galloway and Highland.

Unemployment by region

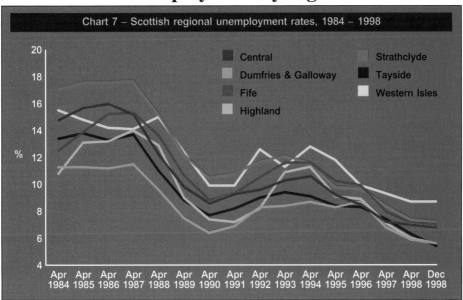

Source: ONS, data supplied by NOMIS

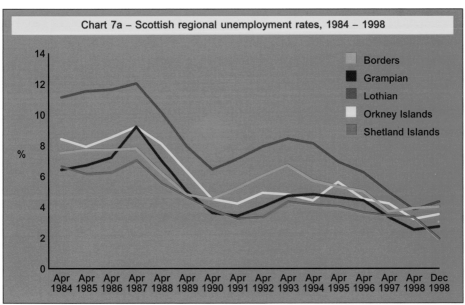

Source: ONS, data supplied by NOMIS

Regional aid

UK Regional Selective Assistance (RSA) is available in varying forms for companies and activities in different parts of Scotland. The assisted areas map – at present under review – is opposite. This divides the UK as a whole into 'development areas' – i.e. qualifying as eligible for the highest levels of assistance – or 'intermediate areas' – the next in line – or non-assisted areas. The map is based upon Travel to Work Areas (TTWA), units significantly smaller than the Scottish regions.

As a special concession, all of the area covered by Highlands and Islands Enterprise (HIE) is effectively granted development area status. Consequently HIE can offer levels of assistance equivalent to those available under RSA, even in those parts of its overall area which do not qualify in their own right.

There have been other 'special' areas of various types over the years, qualifying for special treatment under a variety of programmes and policies. These included the Scottish New Town Development Corporations (Cumbernauld, East Kilbride, Irvine, Glenrothes and Livingston), which are now all wound up. Only one Enterprise Zone (EZ) remains in existence in Scotland, in Lanarkshire. Companies locating there also qualify for special incentives. The Lanarkshire EZ is due to 'expire' formally on 31 January 2003. The Inverclyde EZ expired in March 1999.

Rural Scotland and declining industrial areas have benefited from a variety of EU programmes. In particular the Highlands and Islands Enterprise area has been classified as qualifying for Objective 1 status, reserved for regions with less than 75 per cent of EU average income per head. In the future, Scotland is unlikely to benefit as much from Structural Funds as in the past. It was determined in March 1999 that Objective 1 status for the Highlands & Islands would be removed. However, in recognition of the particular structural problems in that area, a total of 300 million euros (approximately £200 million) was allocated by way of a 'phasing out' programme.

Area aid at a glance

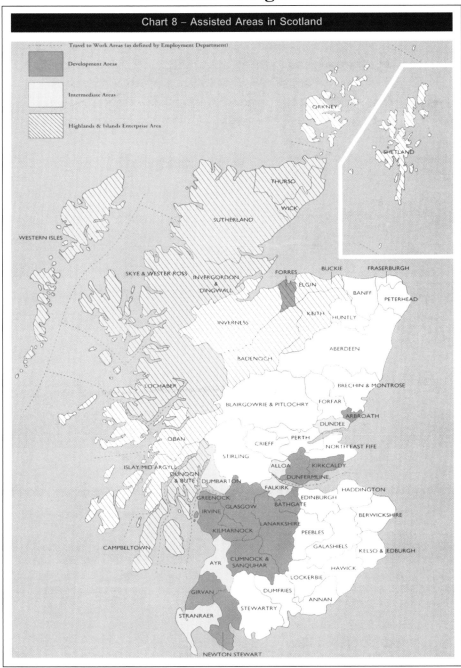

Exports and inward investment

Finally, consider the extent to which these regions are outward looking. Chart 9 shows, for the new local authority areas in 1996, the percentage of total manufacturing employment in their areas which was accounted for by overseas-owned units. Inverclyde, West Lothian and Renfrewshire lead the way – with factors such as New Towns and electronics focus helping to explain their predominance. Other areas with relatively high concentrations of overseas-owned plants include South Lanarkshire, South Ayrshire, Dundee City and West Dunbartonshire.

In terms of absolute numbers employed in these foreign-owned plants, South Lanarkshire and West Lothian lead, followed by Fife and Inverclyde. Overall, in 1996, some 81,750 Scots were employed in 330 overseas-owned manufacturing units, accounting for 29 per cent of total manufacturing employment.

Data from the Scottish Council Development and Industry – with a somewhat different regional split based on the Enterprise company network – shows Renfrewshire as far and away the most significant Scottish area in terms of exports of manufactured goods. Next in line come Lothian and Ayrshire. The only other manufactured goods exporters of any substance are Lanarkshire and the Forth Valley.

For these regions Table 2 shows the major export markets. Information is also available on the top industrial products involved. Thus, in Renfrewshire electronics equipment exports dominate totally, with France followed by Germany as the key markets. The main exports from the Lothians were radio, TV and communications equipment plus office machinery; with France, the Netherlands and the US markets mattering most.

Working for foreign investors

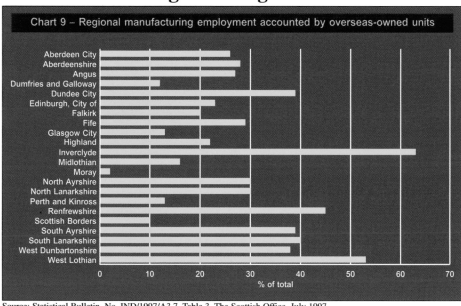

Chart 9 – Regional manufacturing employment accounted by overseas-owned units

Source: Statistical Bulletin, No. IND/1997/A3.7, Table 3, The Scottish Office, July 1997

Who buys what?

Region	Market	1995	1996	Region	Market	1995	1996
Scotland wide	France	2,964	2,804	Grampian	France	84	72
	Germany	1,938	*		Germany	70	*
	US	*	2,224		US	*	64
Highlands &	France	81	117	Tayside	US	†	†
Islands	US	55	156		Norway	†	†
Dunbartonshire	Netherlands	115	98	Forth Valley	Germany	244	261
	US	104	108		France	138	*
Glasgow	Malaysia	86	*		US	*	174
	Norway	58	95	Lothian	France	477	*
	Qatar	*	40		Netherlands	354	442
Renfrewshire	France	1,405	1,524		US	*	422
	Germany	485	532	Borders	Germany	45	38
Ayrshire	Germany	261	*		US	28	*
	US	214	520		France	*	50
	Netherlands	*	381	Lanarkshire	Germany	364	310
Dumfries &	France	†	†		Netherlands	171	221
Galloway	Germany	†	†	* not one of top two markets in this year			
	Italy	†	†	† Data unavailable for disclosure			

Table 2 – Top export markets by region, 1995 and 1996 (£000s)

Source: Scottish Manufacturing and Exports 1996-97, Scottish Council Development and Industry

The regional picture

The data presented in this chapter demonstrate the diverse nature of the Scottish economy. The preponderance of economic activity and employment is in the central belt. However, even here, while there are similarities in terms of economic structure and performance between (for example) Central Region, Fife and Strathclyde, there are also major differences between (for example) Strathclyde and the Lothians.

Grampian Region has the highest GDP per head, generally highest earnings and lowest unemployment. The benefits of the (relative) proximity to offshore oil production and exploration and associated onshore activity is clear. For example, the gap between Grampian and Tayside in both GDP per head and average earnings has widened substantially in recent years.

Orkney and Shetland have also gained from being the base for some onshore activities related to the North Sea oil and gas fields. While separate GDP per head and average earnings data are not available, the difference in unemployment rates between the northern and Western Isles is stark. One consequence of these factors is that population has been increasing in the northern isles and declining in the Western Isles.

The Highlands have a lower unemployment rate than the Western Isles, and population has been growing in absolute numbers and relative to Scotland as a whole. The efforts of HIE (and its predecessor the Highlands and Islands Development Board) to generate a more diverse economic structure have been aided by the assistance available from UK Government and the EU.

Like the Highlands and Islands, the southern regions – Borders and Dumfries and Galloway – represent a small, albeit increasing, percentage of the Scottish population. As difficulties mount for the agricultural and related sectors, so there are signs of relative affluence declining and relative unemployment rising.

Of course there are also many similarities, but the differences will continue – and bring strength to the Scottish economy as a whole. Any discussion would be incomplete without noting at least the essential differences and stressing the rich diversity that it contains.

5

Scottish business

by Jeremy Peat and Stephen Boyle

A lack of companies

Successful modern economies are built on thriving companies. Much of
the dynamism, growth and jobs in western economies in recent years have
come from new and small firms. So companies and a country's ability to
generate them matter. If this aspect of Scotland's performance is poor, we have
a problem.

According to Crawford Beveridge, Chief Executive of Scottish Enterprise,
Scotland does have such a problem. Following a study on business formation,
he concluded: "for some years, perhaps decades, we in Scotland have been
aware that as a nation we seem to have lost some of that entrepreneurial drive
for which the Scots were once famed… it is apparent that we have
a fundamental problem. That problem can be traced back to a simple lack of
companies in Scotland."[1]

Chart 1 appears to support the charge. All firms with a turnover above
a certain threshold have to register with Customs & Excise for Value Added
Tax (VAT) purposes. In 1997 the figure was £49,000 and there were over
117,000 VAT-registered businesses in Scotland, 229 for every 10,000 people.
The equivalent RGB figure was 20 per cent higher: 274 businesses for every
10,000 people. If Scotland had matched the RGB rate there would have been
an extra 23,000 firms, bringing the total to more than 140,000.

Clearly this is not a new phenomenon. In each year from 1985 to 1997,
Scotland's business stock relative to population was less than in RGB.
The gap is smaller now than in the early 1990s but it remains substantial.
On the basis of these figures, Scotland certainly has a "lack of companies",
compared with its most immediate peer group in RGB.

The question is why? There are two possible explanations: a low business
birth rate or a high business death rate. Scotland's business birth rate is
unquestionably low when measured in relation to population. In 1997,
24 new firms were registered for VAT purposes in Scotland for every

1. Crawford W Beveridge: *Scotland's Business Birth Rate,* Scottish Enterprise and Scottish Business Insider, 1993

Business shy in Scotland?

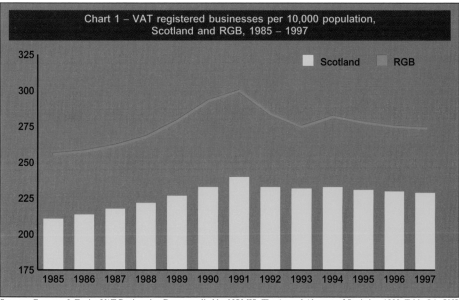

Chart 1 – VAT registered businesses per 10,000 population, Scotland and RGB, 1985 – 1997

Sources: Customs & Excise VAT Registration Data, supplied by NOMIS; The Annual Abstract of Statistics, 1999, Table 5.1, ONS

Trailing GB in start-ups

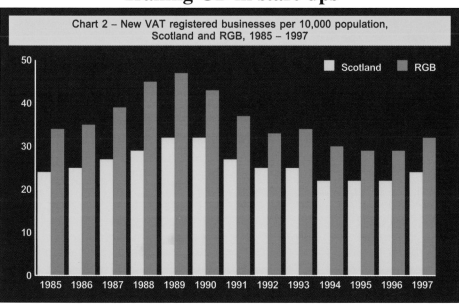

Chart 2 – New VAT registered businesses per 10,000 population, Scotland and RGB, 1985 – 1997

Sources: Customs & Excise VAT Registration Data, supplied by NOMIS; The Annual Abstract of Statistics, 1999, Table 5.1, ONS

10,000 people. The RGB rate was one-third higher at 32 per 10,000 people. So, in 1997, 12,000 new firms were created in Scotland. If we had performed up to the RGB mark the figure would have been more than 16,000.

This appears to be a persistent and long-standing problem. The start-up rate gap compared with RGB is lower than in the 1980s but has barely moved throughout the 1990s. The gap is so substantial that if Scotland had attained the RGB start-up rate between 1985 and 1997 it would have created 67,000 more firms than it did.

This low business birth rate relative to population may be due to historical reasons. Might Scotland do well in creating firms given the size of the existing company base? Chart 3 shows the birth rate as a proportion of the existing stock of firms and it repeats the now familiar tale. It shows that Scotland's birth rate has consistently been below the RGB rate, although by a smaller margin than on the population-adjusted basis. So, if we had achieved the RGB rate in 1997, there would have been almost 14,000 new firms against the 12,000 created. Again, if the RGB rate had been attained between 1985 and 1997 there would have been more than 25,000 extra new starts.

This low business birth rate is thus a major cause of the relatively low number of firms in Scotland. But what of the death rate? The performance here is slightly more encouraging, as Chart 4 illustrates. In 1997, 23 businesses were de-registered in Scotland for every 10,000 people. A VAT de-registration is treated as a business 'death'. This compared with a business death rate in RGB of 29 per 10,000 people, more than 26 per cent greater than in Scotland. Expressed as a percentage of the existing stock of firms, the Scottish rate was less than 10 per cent while the RGB rate was more than 10 per cent. The chart confirms that Scotland's business death rate has consistently been below the RGB rate, although the difference is less than in the case of the birth rate.

Scotland has fewer businesses in relation to its size compared with the RGB, but those started in Scotland are a little less likely to die than firms started elsewhere in GB. The reason for the relatively small business base is simply that Scotland does not create enough new companies and has not done so for many years.

Business replenishment

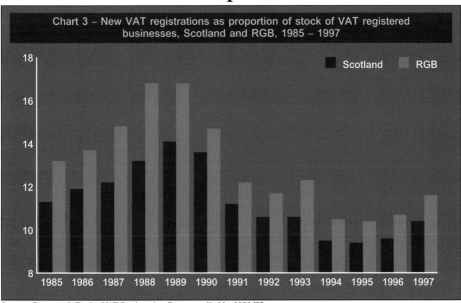

Source: Customs & Excise VAT Registration Data, supplied by NOMIS

Bowing out

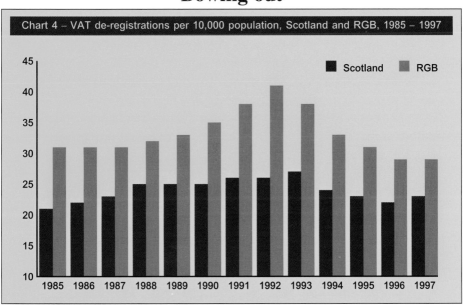

Sources: Customs & Excise VAT Registration Data, supplied by NOMIS, The Annual Abstract of Statistics, 1999, Table 5.1, ONS

Considerable effort has been spent trying to explain why so few of the sons and daughters of Adam Smith set up businesses in Scotland (though many émigrés have done so outside, particularly in North America). The only 'hard' evidence separating Scotland from RGB is that Scots may have found it harder to obtain finance. This is a complex point. For example, Brian Ashcroft shows in Chapter 6 that Scots are less likely than people in RUK to own their own homes. A house is an asset that can be used as security when borrowing from a bank. Since fewer Scots have traditionally been homeowners, they may not have had access to the capital to start-up a business.

A curious regional divide

There is a distinct regional variation in the size of the business base and birth rate across Scotland. The stock of firms per 10,000 people is generally highest in rural and peripheral areas such as the islands, Highlands, Borders and Dumfries and Galloway. Rates here exceed 300 firms per 10,000 people, well above the RGB rate. In contrast, the business base tends to be smallest in the central belt. Places such as Lanarkshire, Dunbartonshire, Falkirk, Renfrewshire, Fife, Glasgow and Dundee all have rates below 200 per 10,000 people. On the face of it, Scotland's problem is an urban one.

The urban-rural split is consistent with another explanation of Scotland's low business birth rate. According to this, decades spent in large workplaces like shipyards, engineering shops, steel plants and local authorities bred an 'employment culture' rather than an entrepreneurial one. It is precisely in the urban central belt that this caricature of Scotland's economic history is most true.

Where the firms are

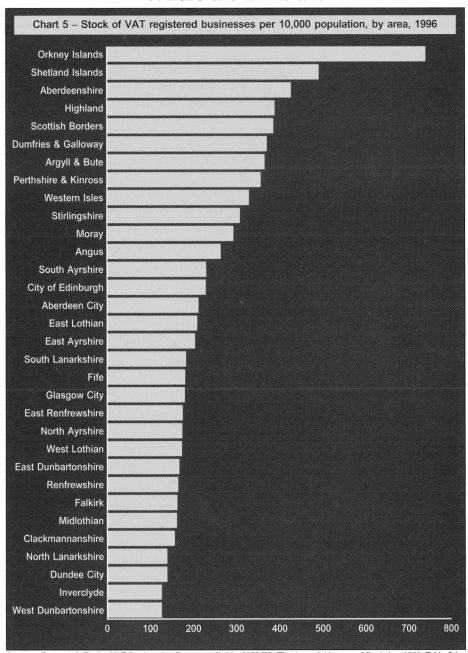

Chart 5 – Stock of VAT registered businesses per 10,000 population, by area, 1996

Sources: Customs & Excise VAT Registration Data, supplied by NOMIS, The Annual Abstract of Statistics, 1999, Table 5.1, ONS

However, if these cultural influences were important in the past there are signs that they may be waning. Chart 6 shows that the business birth rate as a proportion of the stock is currently highest in urban and central belt locations. In 1997 it was highest in the four cities and in places like North Lanarkshire, West Lothian, Dunbartonshire and Renfrewshire. The lowest start-up rates were recorded in the rural and peripheral regions where the stock of businesses is highest.

How Scottish firms perform

Scotland's poor business birth rate is an important issue. If it had been higher there could have been significant benefits in terms of income and jobs. However, it is not the only issue. As well as the number of firms, how well they perform is crucial to our well-being. Here the messages are mixed, but there are some distinctly positive features.

Productivity levels determine how well-off we are and productivity growth determines how quickly we become better-off. The messages in Chart 7 are, therefore, encouraging. Between 1991 and 1996, the value of output per person employed in Scottish manufacturing rose by over 47 per cent compared with just 40 per cent in the UK as a whole. In fact, labour productivity in Scotland rose faster than in any other part of the UK during that period and in 1996 was higher than in any other area except Wales. This strong performance is evident across a range of industries, but most so in electronics where inward investors have achieved a productivity performance well in excess of that of indigenous businesses. In general, as Neil Hood shows in Chapter 3, productivity levels are highest in foreign-owned plants.

Where new businesses are

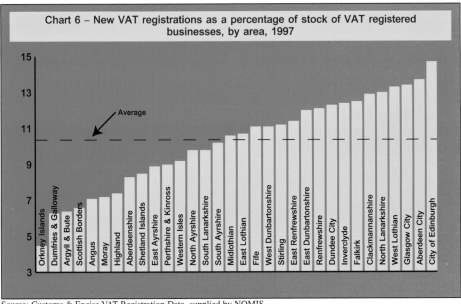

Source: Customs & Excise VAT Registration Data, supplied by NOMIS

Adding value

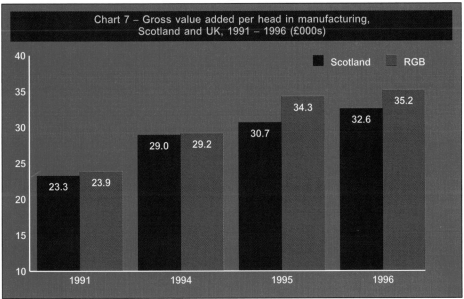

Source: ONS, Regional Competitiveness Indicators

Of course, manufacturing is only one part of the economy. Making judgements about labour productivity for the whole economy is more difficult, but Chart 8 makes a fairly robust comparison between Scotland and the RUK. Again the conclusions are favourable to Scotland. Between 1990 and 1996, output per person in employment rose at a slightly faster rate than in the RUK and in 1996 output per person in Scotland was marginally above the RUK figure.

Unfortunately, as far as productivity is concerned, Scotland might just be a good team in a bad league. Research carried out by the McKinsey Global Institute shows that between 1994 and 1996, UK labour productivity was 21 per cent lower than in West Germany and France and 27 per cent lower than in the United States. Scotland needs to boost its labour productivity level considerably if it is to achieve income levels comparable with the world's best.

Scotland invests for the future

Investment is the seed that firms, government and individuals sow today to reap by way of higher incomes later. It is quite possible to have too much investment – the lessons of South East Asia are still fresh – but few have argued in recent years that it is Britain's problem. What about Scotland? Chart 9 shows that Scotland has generally done fairly well as compared with the RUK. Measured as a proportion of GDP, investment in Scotland exceeded the UK rate in three out of four years in the first half of the 1990s. The information is limited, omitting investment in people through education and training, for example, but it provides some encouraging reading.

Research and development (R&D) is a particularly important form of investment. The ability to innovate, to develop new products, processes and services is crucial for a company if it is to retain or enhance its competitiveness. Extensive innovative activity in an economy is also likely to mean more well paid and highly skilled jobs.

How productivity compares...

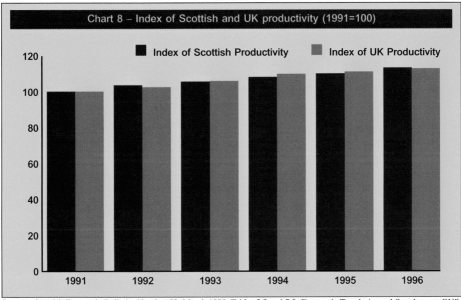

Chart 8 – Index of Scottish and UK productivity (1991=100)

Sources: Scottish Economic Bulletin, Number 59, March 1999, Tables 2.2 and 7.2; Economic Trends Annual Supplement, ONS

...and investment

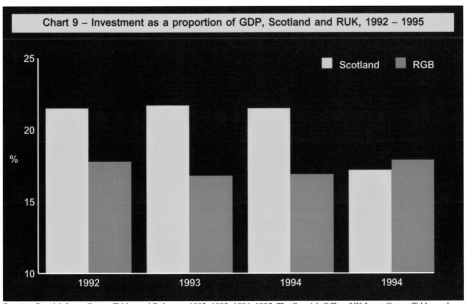

Chart 9 – Investment as a proportion of GDP, Scotland and RUK, 1992 – 1995

Sources: Scottish Input-Output Tables and Balances, 1992, 1993, 1994, 1995, The Scottish Office; UK Input-Output Tables and Balances, 1992, 1993, 1994, 1995, ONS; Regional Trends 33, 1998, Table 2.1, ONS

Unfortunately, as Chart 10 shows, the level of business R&D in Scotland is notably low as compared with the RUK. Business R&D in Scotland was only 0.6 per cent of GDP in 1996, less than half of the UK rate. As Chart 11 illustrates, the only sector in which Scotland's share of business R&D exceeds its share of UK GDP is 'electrical machinery', in other words, electronics. It is quite understandable that in some industries – like transport equipment and aerospace – our share of R&D is small because these industries are not very important in Scotland. However, it is worrying that our share of overall manufacturing and services R&D is so paltry.

Why? The answer does not appear to be the availability of the necessary skills, since Scotland's universities account for over 12 per cent of UK R&D in higher education institutions. It is more likely to be a combination of our industrial mix – if the transport equipment industry is small, so too will be Scotland's share of transport R&D – and the structure of ownership in the Scottish economy. R&D is a high-level function and often a 'headquarters' one. A company's R&D effort is central to its future and devolving it to a subsidiary is a major step. There are some excellent examples in Scotland – Hewlett Packard's South Queensferry site holds one of the company's 'global mandates' for R&D – but not many. If there were more headquarters functions the story would be different. However, there has been a notable change in the 1990s.

What a difference a decade makes

In the 1980s, no respectable conversation about the state of Scottish business was complete without some ritual breast-beating about the 'threat' of external take-overs. However, the 1990s have seen a significant redrawing of Scotland's corporate landscape. One example is the number of Financial Times Stock Exchange (FTSE) listed firms headquartered in Scotland now compared with 10 years ago.

Scotland's R&D gap

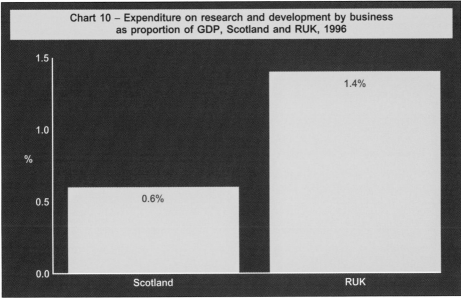

Chart 10 – Expenditure on research and development by business as proportion of GDP, Scotland and RUK, 1996

Source: Regional Trends 33, 1998, Table 13.8, ONS

Where R&D is trailing

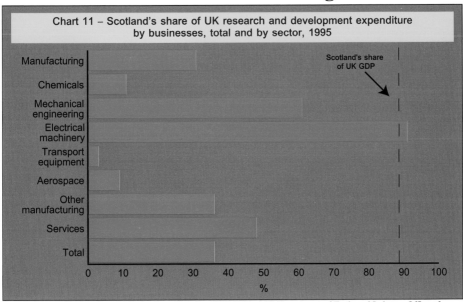

Chart 11 – Scotland's share of UK research and development expenditure by businesses, total and by sector, 1995

Source: Science, Engineering and Technology Statistics, 1997, Table 4.10, Department of Trade and Industry, Office of Science and Technology

On that measure, Chart 12 makes impressive reading. In 1989 there were only three Scottish firms in the FTSE 100 list of the UK's biggest companies: The Royal Bank of Scotland, Scottish & Newcastle (S&N) and Burmah, although the last of these was Scottish in name only. Ten years later the total had risen to seven, much closer to Scotland's share of UK population and UK GDP. Burmah has gone and The Royal Bank of Scotland and S&N have been joined by Stagecoach, Scottish & Southern Energy, Scottish Power, British Energy and Bank of Scotland.

The striking feature is that most of the additions are the result of changes in government policy, specifically the privatisation and restructuring of the electricity industry and the liberalisation of the bus, coach and rail sectors. These reforms did more than change the nameplates on the doors. They gave the opportunity to transform public sector bodies into thriving companies.

Chart 12 demonstrates that Scottish firms have also become more prominent beyond the FTSE 100. There are now 25 Scottish companies in the FTSE 250 – 10 per cent of the total – compared with only four in 1989. Scottish firms account for more than 15 per cent of companies in the FTSE 250 outside the top 100.

The other notable aspect of the last decade has been the reversal of roles. There will always be take-overs of Scottish firms from outside Scotland, but the 1990s have seen the emergence of a number of Scottish firms which are more than adept at doing the acquiring themselves. Examples include Stagecoach – with businesses throughout the UK and in Europe, Africa and beyond – Scottish Power with its US operation, The Royal Bank of Scotland which owns Citizens Bank in New England and Angel Trains, Weir Group with acquisitions in several countries and Scottish Media Group which has interests throughout the UK.

Some significant strengths, but could do better

Crawford Beveridge was undoubtedly correct: Scotland produces too few firms. If Scotland had managed to achieve the RGB's rate of new firm formation there would have been many more businesses and, probably, higher income and employment levels. While attending to this deficiency is clearly a policy priority, two points must be borne in mind. First, if there is some kind of 'entrepreneurial deficit' in Scotland, its roots are deep in culture, history and economics. They cannot be eradicated in only a few years. Rather, a sustained programme of measures over decades will be required if Scotland is, first, to match and then to exceed the RGB.

Second, there are some particularly encouraging aspects of the performance of Scottish business in the 1990s. Compared with the RUK, productivity growth and investment performance have been strong, although there is a clear weakness in R&D. Scotland is now also home to some very significant businesses. It supports the headquarters functions of seven FTSE 100 companies, something which would have been inconceivable only a decade ago. What is more, they are successful companies.

The lesson of the 1990s is that Scotland can be the home of prominent and thriving companies. The challenge for the next decade is to make it home to more firms which achieve high and rising levels of productivity.

League promotion

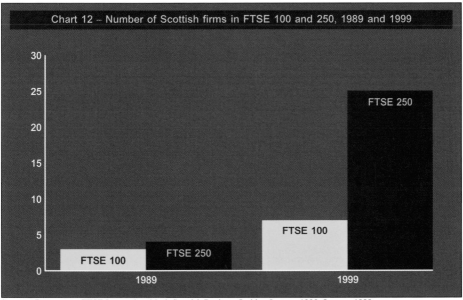

Chart 12 – Number of Scottish firms in FTSE 100 and 250, 1989 and 1999

Sources: Datastream; FTSE International Ltd; Scottish Business Insider, January 1990, January 1999

6

Scotland's households

by Brian Ashcroft

We are all consumers now, even the Scots! A walk down Glasgow's Argyle Street on a Saturday afternoon quickly reveals the scale and importance of consumer activity.

New shops, shopping centres and out-of-town shopping malls provide further evidence of the importance of consumption to the everyday lives of most Scots. Consumption is now a social, as well as an economic and commercial, activity. The traditional sight of the disgruntled husband being dragged around the shops has been replaced by an image of shopping as leisure pursuit. So, cafés are married to bookshops, fashion stores incorporate video screens that pump out rock music. Even betting shops offer more salubrious surroundings.

Of course, consumption is about more than shopping. But the 'shopping revolution' is a clear manifestation of the rising expenditure, incomes and wealth enjoyed by the Scottish consumer over the past decade.

How we spend in Scotland

Chart 1 shows how spending by the average Scottish household increased by about 5 per cent in real terms over the eight years after 1988/89. The increase broadly parallels that in the UK. But as the chart indicates, this growth was not constant. In some years expenditure fell and then rose, reflecting the fortunes of the broader economy in both Scotland and the UK as a whole.

However, Scots spend less than their counterparts south of the border. While the spending of the average Scottish household approached that of the UK in 1993 and 1994/95, it seems likely that this narrowing was due to changes in the method of data collection rather than an economic phenomenon. Generally, for every pound spent by the average UK household, Scots spent about 90p.

The rise in weekly spending

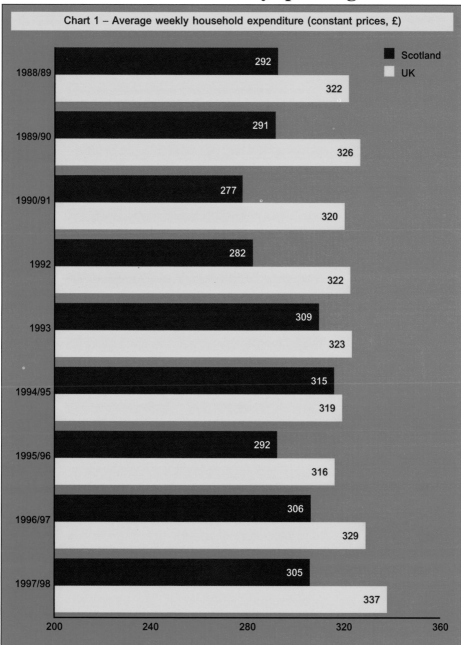

Chart 1 – Average weekly household expenditure (constant prices, £)

	Scotland	UK
1988/89	292	322
1989/90	291	326
1990/91	277	320
1992	282	322
1993	309	323
1994/95	315	319
1995/96	292	316
1996/97	306	329
1997/98	305	337

Sources: Family Spending, ONS; Scottish Economic Bulletin, 1988-1999, The Scottish Office; Family Expenditure Survey in Regional Trends, 1988-1998, ONS

Is this an example of the legendary thriftiness (or tight-fistedness), of the Scots? Not really. The Scots are on average less well-off than their counterparts in the rest of the UK. In 1995/96, the average gross weekly income of the Scottish household was £338, more than 10 per cent below the average for the UK. Chart 2 reveals that, if anything, Scots spend a greater proportion of their income than the average UK household. Over the eight years shown, household spending averaged 76 per cent of income in Scotland against 75 per cent for the UK.

If the Scots spend less than the average UK family, do they also spend their income differently? Chart 3 suggests that they do.

The message here is that Scots spend proportionately more of their income on smoking, drinking, eating, using public transport and heating their homes. However, proportionately less is spent on housing, furnishing the home, motoring, personal goods and services, and leisure activities.

Some of the difference is due to the lower level of family income in Scotland. This probably accounts for the higher percentage of outlays on food, public transport and heating, and the smaller shares spent on furnishings, motoring and leisure expenditures. However, the lower proportional spend on housing almost certainly reflects differences in the structure of the housing market in Scotland, with its relatively lower incidence of owner occupation.

But despite lower incomes, Scots' households actually spent more than their UK counterparts in two areas in 1997/98. First, £8 per week is spent on smoking as against £6 in the UK, while £14 per week is spent on heating the home, compared to £13 in the UK – a clear reflection of the colder Scottish winter weather.

Tight-fisted? Don't believe it

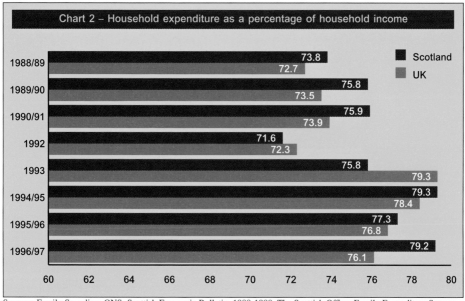

Sources: Family Spending, ONS; Scottish Economic Bulletin, 1988-1999, The Scottish Office; Family Expenditure Survey in Regional Trends, 1988-1998, ONS

Where the money goes

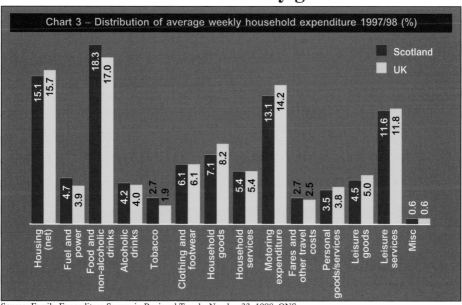

Source: Family Expenditure Survey in Regional Trends, Number 33, 1998, ONS

Chart 4 shows the spending patterns of Scottish and UK households ten years ago. What is clear is that rising incomes have reduced the proportion of income spent on 'essentials' such as housing, heating, food, drink and clothing, while the percentage spent on 'luxuries' has risen. Motoring and leisure services are prime examples of this category.

Income patterns in Scotland

Wages and salaries are the principal source of household income. In 1995/96, they accounted for about 59 per cent of Scottish household income compared to 57 per cent in the UK. Of the remaining sources of income, social security payments were by far the most important. They accounted for 27 per cent of Scottish and 26 per cent of UK household income, an indication of marginally lower incomes and higher unemployment in Scotland.

Income from self-employment and savings contributed less to Scottish household income than in the UK as a whole. Income from self-employment contributed 7 per cent to the average income of Scottish households against a contribution of nearly 9 per cent for the whole of the UK, possibly reflecting a relatively lower level of small business activity. And, with income from savings instruments contributing less than 6 per cent against 7 per cent for the UK overall, we have a further indication that the Scots may not be as thrifty as music hall legend suggests. However, this could reflect a relatively lower capacity to save out of income, a preference for long-term saving through life assurance endowment policies, and the greater incidence of employment in the public sector, with relatively higher job security and unfunded pension benefits.

Where we spent in the past

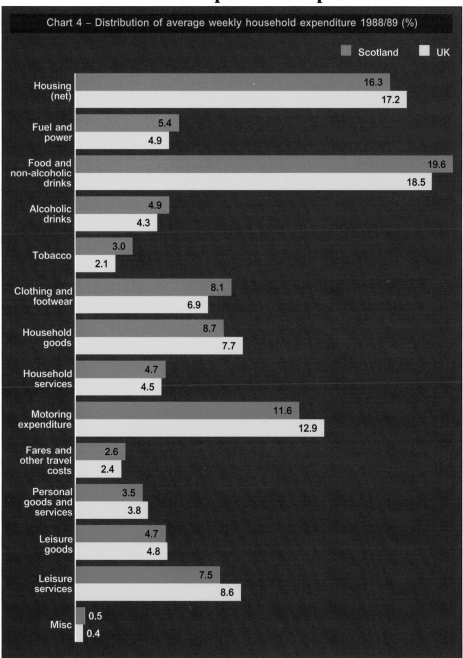

Chart 4 – Distribution of average weekly household expenditure 1988/89 (%)

Scotland   UK

	Scotland	UK
Housing (net)	16.3	17.2
Fuel and power	5.4	4.9
Food and non-alcoholic drinks	19.6	18.5
Alcoholic drinks	4.9	4.3
Tobacco	3.0	2.1
Clothing and footwear	8.1	6.9
Household goods	8.7	7.7
Household services	4.7	4.5
Motoring expenditure	11.6	12.9
Fares and other travel costs	2.6	2.4
Personal goods and services	3.5	3.8
Leisure goods	4.7	4.8
Leisure services	7.5	8.6
Misc	0.5	0.4

Source: Scottish Economic Bulletin, Number 42, December 1990, Table 5.1, page 74

In 1997, the average gross weekly earnings of full-time male employees in Scotland amounted to £378, or about £19,000 per year. For male employees in Great Britain (GB) the equivalent figures were £406 per week, or more than £21,000 per year. Chart 5 shows that both males and females enjoyed a real increase in earnings between 1986 and 1997. Scottish male employees experienced real earnings growth of about 17 per cent over the period. For GB as a whole the increase was 22 per cent. Female employees enjoyed even greater real increases – 23 per cent in Scotland and 34 per cent in GB as a whole. These growth rates reflect, inter alia, the stronger growth of earnings in the service sector in the south east of England and the City of London in particular.

Female workers still receive less than men. In 1997, male employees in Scotland and GB as a whole received on average more than one third as much again as their female counterparts. However, as Chart 6 shows, the relative position of females has progressively improved over the last decade. In 1986, full-time male employees received earnings which were more than half again as great as the earnings of full-time females. The relative improvement in female earnings has been faster in Scotland since 1986, with the ratio falling by 11 per cent compared to 9 per cent in Britain. But the gap between male and female earnings still continues to be greater in Scotland.

Employment earnings depend on more than gender. Type of occupation, industry and even location all have an influence. The innate desire for self-improvement through education and skills enhancement is rewarded, as elsewhere, by higher earnings.

The rise and rise of earnings

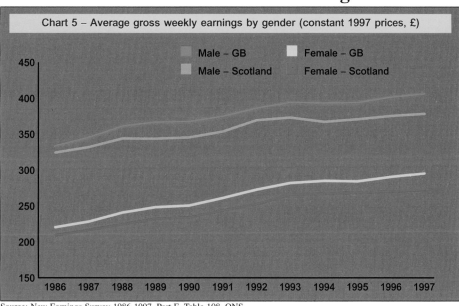

Source: New Earnings Survey 1986-1997, Part E, Table 108, ONS

Women catching up

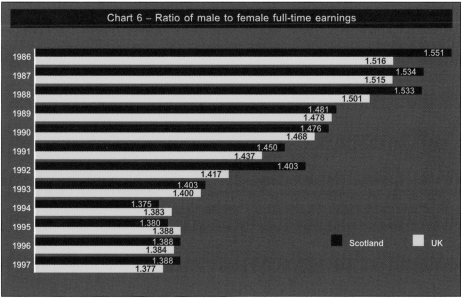

Source: New Earnings Survey 1986-1997, Part E, Table 108, ONS

Chart 7 highlights the differences in average gross weekly earnings in 1998 by occupational group. Male managers and administrators do best. Their weekly earnings are, at £573, more than twice as high as males in 'other occupations', the category with the lowest weekly average. Professionals are the next best rewarded, followed by associate professionals, craft and related, personal and protective services, plant and machine operatives, sales, and clerical and secretarial.

But it is evident that the gender gap in earnings persists in all occupational categories. Across all occupations the gap is 30 per cent, which means that females received on average about 70 per cent of male earnings.

The biggest gaps are to be found in the traditionally male jobs such as craft and related, and personal and protective services, where female earnings are 40 per cent and 38 per cent lower respectively. But clerical and secretarial occupations, traditionally seen as jobs for women, have the narrowest gap of 16 per cent. Professional occupations have, at 20 per cent, one of the smallest gaps, reflecting the 'equal pay for similar work' policies in many organisations. However, the gender gap of 35 per cent in the average earnings of managers and administrators is surprising and suggests that the 'glass ceiling' is as firmly in place in Scotland as elsewhere.

Differences in average industrial earnings are also quite marked. These are shown in Chart 8. Male non-manual workers in financial services receive gross weekly earnings of £519, while female manual workers in hotels and restaurants receive only £157 per week. The incidence of low pay amongst male manual workers is particularly evident in hotels and restaurants, and other community, social and personal service activities. Earnings in the wholesale and retail trade are also low, particularly in the male and female non-manual categories. Generally, employees in all categories earn more on average in manufacturing industries than in services, with the earnings of female manual workers in service industries being especially low.

Who earns how much

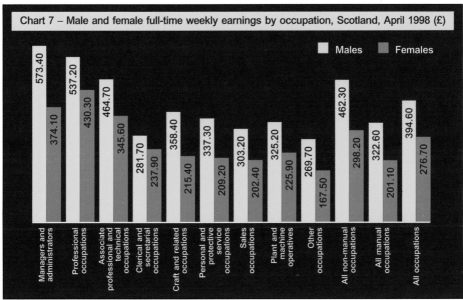

Chart 7 – Male and female full-time weekly earnings by occupation, Scotland, April 1998 (£)

Source: New Earnings Survey 1998, Part E, Table E13, ONS

How weekly pay differs

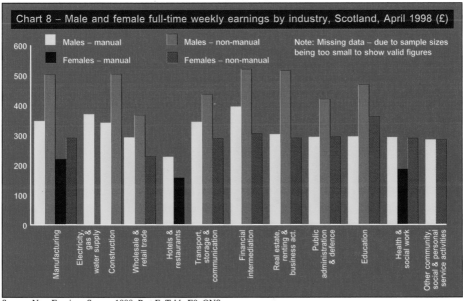

Chart 8 – Male and female full-time weekly earnings by industry, Scotland, April 1998 (£)

Source: New Earnings Survey 1998, Part E, Table E9, ONS

Chart 9 reveals the variation across the regions of Scotland in average gross weekly earnings in 1996. Lothian and Strathclyde are closest to the Scottish averages of £375 for full-time males and £270 for females. This is mainly because the concentration of employees in these regions dominates the Scottish averages.

Earnings are lowest in the rural areas of Dumfries and Galloway and (although not reported), probably also in the Borders and Highlands and Islands. The highest male earnings are found in Grampian, while female earnings are highest in Lothian. The industrial and occupational composition of the Scottish regions is principally responsible for the differences: manual occupations in agriculture in rural areas, oil industry activities in Grampian and non-manual jobs in financial services in Lothian. But it is likely that there are also regional specific effects with, for example, earnings tending to be generally higher in Grampian due to the stronger overall growth shown by the region.

A final insight into the variation in employee earnings in Scotland is provided by Chart 10 which presents the cumulative distribution of gross hourly earnings for both males and females in Scotland and GB as a whole as at April 1998. The graph highlights the greater incidence of low pay amongst females in Scotland, where 1.5 per cent earn less than £2.90 per hour against 0.9 per cent in GB. At the other extreme, a much greater proportion of employees in GB overall earn more than £15 per hour. Around 16 per cent of males and 8 per cent of females in GB, compared to 13 per cent of males and less than 6 per cent of females in Scotland, receive hourly earnings in this band.

In both Scotland and GB overall, the greatest proportions of employees earn between £5 and £7.50 an hour. However, the proportions in this earnings band are higher in Scotland, with 31 per cent of men and 38 per cent of women in Scotland earning these amounts, against 28 and 34 per cent respectively for GB as a whole. This is principally because the earnings distribution is flatter in GB, reflecting the smaller spread of higher income earners in Scotland.

Pay packets by region

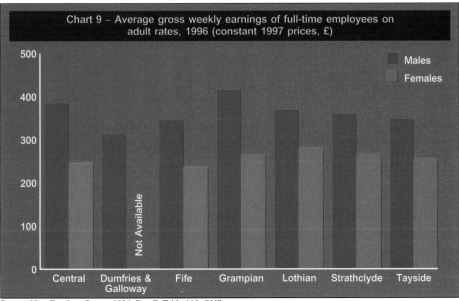

Source: New Earnings Survey 1996, Part E, Table 110, ONS

How Scots earnings compare

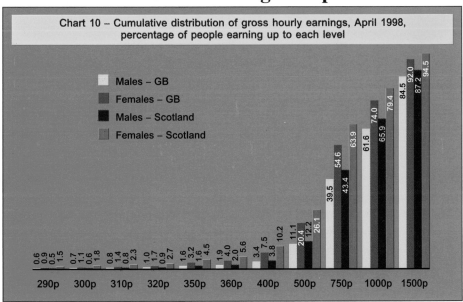

Source: New Earnings Survey 1998, Part E, Table E6, ONS

How Scotland saves

Consumption is fuelled by wealth as well as income. While Scots have a reputation for thrift and saving, the data presented suggest that wealth formation is lower in Scotland than in the UK because of lower incomes.

Estimates of the absolute levels of weekly real (after inflation) household savings in Scotland and the UK are shown in Chart 11. Two facts stand out. First, the level of household savings remained below the UK average between 1987/88 and 1995/96. The one exception is 1993. Second, savings tended to fall in both Scotland and the UK during the period.

However, some caution must be exercised in interpreting these figures. The savings estimates are obtained by subtracting household expenditures from household income. The Family Expenditure Survey, the principal source for these data, measures expenditure on a different basis from the income estimate. And both calculations are subject to statistical errors because they are based on a sample of the population.

While bearing this caveat in mind, a possible explanation for variations in savings behaviour, both over time and between Scotland and the UK, is changes in household income. Chart 12 graphs the ratio of estimated savings to income for Scotland and the UK. The Scottish household savings rate is now closer to the UK rate than the estimates of the absolute levels of savings. This is because incomes are lower in Scotland. Nevertheless, the estimated rates still vary over time. While the expected lower average propensity to save in Scotland is clearly evident, the savings rates in both Scotland and the UK appear to have fallen in the mid-1990s compared to the 1980s.

As a general guide, the savings ratio tends to fall during cyclical upswings in the economy – reflecting greater financial confidence – and rise during periods of economic slowdown. But there are many influences on this particular measure. We cannot be certain whether changes in the ratio are simply a statistical phenomenon or a real change in the savings and expenditure behaviour of UK households. The savings ratio is one of the most complex and ambiguous statistical tools and conclusions drawn from it need to be treated with particular caution.

Putting something by

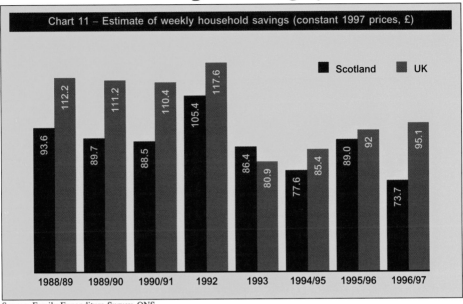

Chart 11 – Estimate of weekly household savings (constant 1997 prices, £)

Source: Family Expenditure Survey, ONS

Saving less than the UK

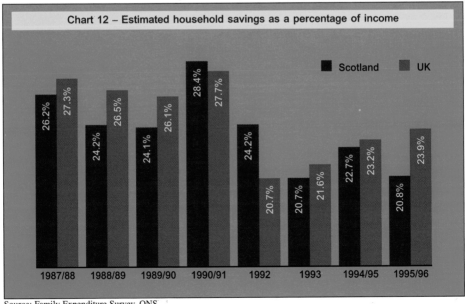

Chart 12 – Estimated household savings as a percentage of income

Source: Family Expenditure Survey, ONS

Data on the household holdings of different types of savings support the view that savings are lower in Scotland. Chart 13 reveals that the proportion of Scottish households holding savings instruments is lower than the overall British level in each instance shown. Bank current accounts and other bank or building society accounts are by far the most popular method of saving in both Scotland and Britain as a whole.

However, Scots appear to be proportionately less likely to hold their savings in National Savings, Premium Bonds, Post Office accounts and Tax Exempt Special Savings Accounts (TESSAs). It is possible that savings in Scotland could be as high as in GB if the smaller number of account holders in Scotland have a sufficiently high savings rate. But unpublished research by Stirling University's David Bell for The Royal Bank of Scotland implies that this is not the case.

Housing in Scotland

Housing forms the major part of the wealth holdings of most households. It also has an important influence on consumer spending. In 1988, for example, equity withdrawal – raising a further loan on the property to finance spending on non-home related items – accounted for 6 per cent of total consumption in the UK. Chart 14 identifies how the housing stock is distributed between the different ownership types.

What stands out is the big difference between Scotland and the rest of GB in the proportions of public rental and owner-occupied housing. Traditionally, the private rented sector and more recently local authority supplied housing played a much bigger role in the housing market in Scotland. A culture of owner-occupation developed much later here. This can still be seen today. Almost 30 per cent of the housing stock in Scotland is provided by local authorities compared to about 19 per cent in GB. Owner-occupation, on the other hand, is confined to 59 per cent of Scottish homes, while in GB 67 per cent of homes are owner-occupied.

House prices are lower in Scotland. In the first three months of 1998, the average house price in Scotland was £66,000 against £79,000 for the UK.

How the Scots save

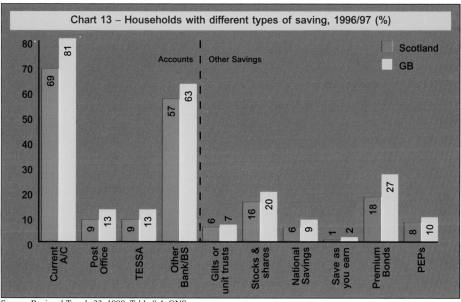

Source: Regional Trends 33, 1998, Table 8.4, ONS

How Scots' housing compares

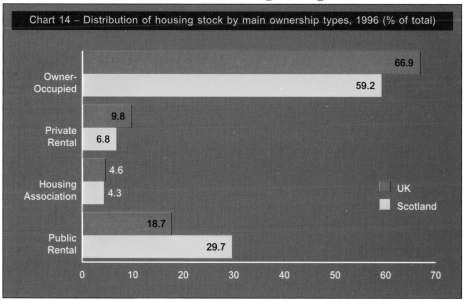

Source: Housing Finance National Market Review 1998, Table 1, Statistical Supplement, Council of Mortgage Lenders

Chart 15 indicates that between 1985 and 1998 house prices in Scotland were consistently below the UK average. Scottish house prices averaged 84 per cent of UK house prices. Indeed, during the UK house price 'boom' of 1988 and 1989, house prices in Scotland fell to 67 per cent of the UK average; an indication that the boom, so marked in the south east of England and Greater London in particular, was hardly felt here. Moreover, housing also appears to be somewhat cheaper in Scotland, with house prices averaging 3.4 times annual household income between 1992 and 1995, compared to a ratio of 3.5 in the UK overall.

The generally lower level of house prices in Scotland has also meant that house buyers need to borrow less to finance their house purchase than their UK counterparts. Chart 16 plots the ratio of mortgage advances to the income of borrowers in Scotland and the UK between 1990 and 1997. The Scottish ratio is consistently lower, with advances averaging 1.9 times income compared to an average of 2.1 for the UK. Scots therefore spend a lower proportion of their incomes on housing and are less burdened by housing debt.

A low rate of home ownership, lower average house prices and a lower burden of housing debt, have several implications for the economy in Scotland. The possibilities for wealth formation, particularly through house price appreciation, are more limited than in the RUK. The low rate of new firm formation in Scotland may in part be a consequence of the limited housing collateral available to raise finance to start new businesses. And the lower burden of housing debt implies that Scottish households are less affected by interest rate changes and fluctuations in UK monetary policy.

Scotland, in short, may continue to converge with the rest of the UK in terms of consumer behaviour. But important differences persist. They spring in the main from lower income and wealth levels. And the reasons for these lie as much in the dynamic performance of London's financial service sector in recent years – which has pushed up the UK averages – as in Scotland's own performance as a host of heavy manufacturing industries went into sharp decline. There seems little to bear out the legend of the 'thrifty Scot'. Equally, the economy in Scotland has been spared the worst of the exuberant excesses that brought policy correction and slowdown in their train.

How house prices have moved

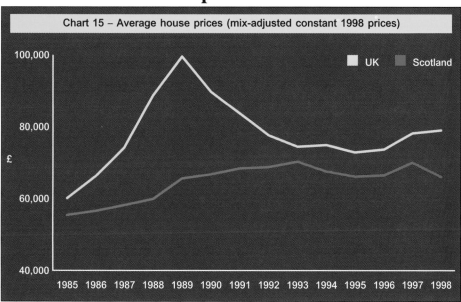

Source: Housing Finance, No 40, Nov 1998, Table 8, Statistical Supplement, Council of Mortgage Lenders

Less keen to gear up

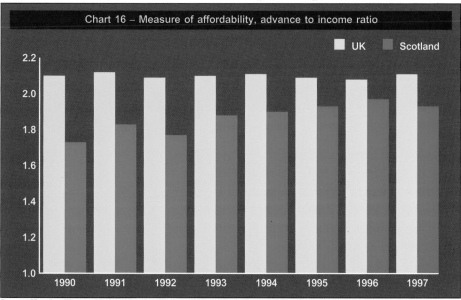

Source: Housing Finance National Market Review 1998, Table 6, Statistical Supplement, Council of Mortgage Lenders

7

Working, learning and training

by Jeremy Peat and Stephen Boyle

In late 1998, the McKinsey Global Institute published an analysis of UK economic performance.[1] It put the UK bottom of the league table of the Group of Seven major industrial nations in terms of output per head and said that poor labour productivity was to blame. One of its recommendations was greater investment in workforce skills and adaptability.

How does Scotland fare? This chapter looks at the jobs we do and at unemployment, and reviews recent evidence on Scotland's ability to meet the 'skills challenge'.

What do we do?

In 1996, there were more than two million employees in Scotland and 250,000 self-employed. Chart 1 demonstrates that working for someone else is more pronounced and self-employment less so than in the rest of GB. Scotland accounted for 9 per cent of GB employees in 1996, but only 7 per cent of the self-employed. This is consistent with evidence of a markedly lower business start-up rate in Scotland (see Chapter 5).

Chart 2 details the ten industries which employed the largest numbers of people. Together they accounted for two-thirds of all employees. Only one of the ten was in manufacturing (food processing and drinks production) and this came in tenth. More people now work in butchers' shops than coal mines, and more than ten times as many repair motor vehicles as make them. The leading employers are health and social work (13 per cent of all employees), retailing (10 per cent), education (8 per cent) and local and central government administration (also 8 per cent).

1. McKinsey Global Institute, Driving productivity and growth in the UK economy, 1998, McKinsey & Company

Hired hands, self-starters

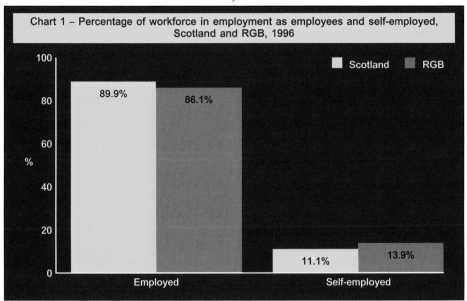

Chart 1 – Percentage of workforce in employment as employees and self-employed, Scotland and RGB, 1996

Sources: Annual Employment Survey, 1996, data supplied by NOMIS; Labour Force Survey, data supplied by NOMIS

Scotland's top 10 employers

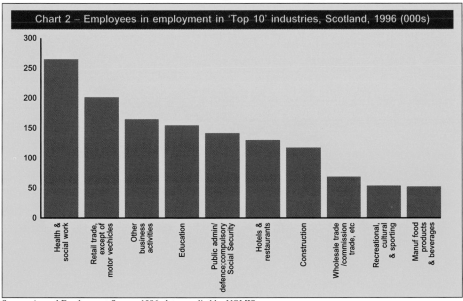

Chart 2 – Employees in employment in 'Top 10' industries, Scotland, 1996 (000s)

Source: Annual Employment Survey, 1996, data supplied by NOMIS

105

The changing pattern of employment

In 1991 and 1996 the total number of employees was almost identical. Gains of 113,000 jobs in 24 sectors, and losses of 109,000 in 31, left a net gain of just under 4,000. Thus, despite the modest aggregate change, the industrial structure altered markedly.

There were substantial numbers of new jobs in health and social work; business services – such as recruitment agencies, accountants and solicitors – shops and computer services. Only one manufacturing sector – our old friend electronics – made the 'top ten' employment growth industries. Total service sector employment rose by 60,000, or 4 per cent. The story was similar for the rest of the UK.

Manufacturing industries are more prominent among the sectors which shed jobs, accounting for six of the 'top ten' for losses. Overall, 40,000 manufacturing jobs were lost, with food and drink, machinery, transport equipment and chemicals to the fore.

The biggest loser of jobs over the period was construction. Employment in this often volatile industry fell by almost 17,000 to 117,000, although much of the change may be due to construction workers moving from employee jobs to self-employment. Land transport – mainly railways, coach services and road haulage – also lost a large number of jobs, falling by 13,000 to 39,000.

So, not only is the service sector dominant, but the shift from manufacturing to services continues.

Looking at industries is one way of analysing employment trends. The other is to look at occupations. Here precise comparisons over time and between Scotland and the rest of GB are problematic. However, Chart 3 points to some clear conclusions. First, between 1992 and 1996, jobs were generally lost in occupations which either require low skill levels – classified as 'unskilled' jobs – or where 'traditional' skills are important, such as craft occupations. Second, demand rose for higher skilled positions – in management and professional jobs – and in personal services such as consultancy and sales.

Employment snakes and ladders

Table 1 – Employment change, selected sectors, Scotland, 1991 – 1996			
Top 10 growth sectors		**Top 10 decline sectors**	
Health and social work	28,800	Construction	-16,900
Other business activities	9,200	Land transport; transport via pipelines	-13,100
Retail trade, except of motor vehicles	9,100	Manuf food products and beverages	-9,500
Sale, maintenance/repair motor vehicles	7,900	Manuf machinery and equipment nec	-9,000
Activities membership organisations nec	7,200	Manuf other transport equipment	-7,500
Computing and related activities	7,000	Education	-6,400
Sewage/refuse disposal, sanitation, etc	6,400	Manuf chemicals and chemical products	-4,400
Supporting/auxiliary transport, etc	5,400	Manuf other non-metallic products	-4,000
Manuf electrical machinery/ apparatus nec	5,300	Insurance and pension funding, etc	-3,600
Agriculture, hunting, etc	5,200	Manuf fabricated metal products, etc	-3,500

Sources: Census of Employment, 1991; Annual Employment Survey, 1996; data supplied by NOMIS

The work we do

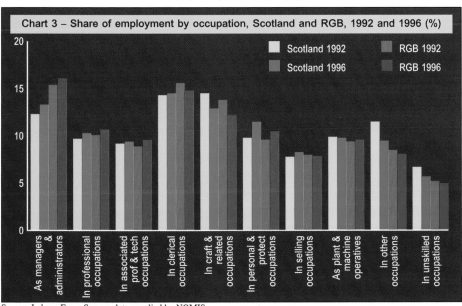

Chart 3 – Share of employment by occupation, Scotland and RGB, 1992 and 1996 (%)

Source: Labour Force Survey, data supplied by NOMIS

These long-term trends apply equally to the rest of GB and other developed economies and show no sign of abating. Importantly, they mean that if Scots are to fill the jobs which become available in the future, we need not only to change the skills we have but also continuously to upgrade them.

Unemployment

Chapter 2 showed that, while the level of unemployment broadly moves in line with economic performance, there has been a clear downward trend since the 1980s. Chart 4 details the proportion of unemployed who have been out of work for more than six months and 12 months in Scotland and the rest of the UK. It shows that the proportion of unemployed people who are out of work 'long-term' has fallen.

In mid-1996, just under half those unemployed in Scotland had been out of work for more than six months and almost 30 per cent for more than one year. So, there has been a significant fall from the 1980s and the recession of the early 1990s. The chart also illustrates the change in Scotland's performance compared with the rest of the UK.

Until the early 1990s, Scotland generally had a higher proportion of people who were 'long-term' unemployed. However, this has changed. The proportion of those unemployed who have been out of work for more than six months and 12 months is higher in the rest of the UK than in Scotland and the difference is quite marked.

While the decline in long-term unemployment is welcome, not all of it is down to improved economic performance. Much of the fall is attributable to the transfer of unemployment benefit claimants to sickness benefits.

Who is unemployed? Chart 5 provides details of the skills characteristics of those out of work in Scotland in 1998. The message is clear: the higher the skill level, the less likely people are to be long-term unemployed. Thus, those who have a university degree or equivalent accounted for

Time out of work

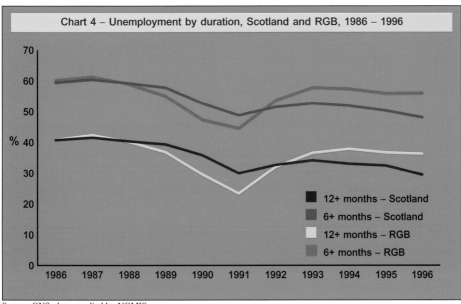

Source: ONS, data supplied by NOMIS

Have skills, can work

Source: Labour Force Survey, Autumn 1998, provided by SPSSMR

around 10 per cent of the unemployed, but only 3 per cent of those who had been out of work for more than a year. By contrast, those who have not attained the equivalent of a Standard Grade pass accounted for 40 per cent of the unemployed and 55 per cent of the long-term unemployed.

Skills matter

Employment data show that demand for labour has shifted from lower skills to higher skills and from 'traditional' to 'new'. All the forecasts predict these trends will continue. The low skilled are more likely to be unemployed for lengthy periods than the highly skilled. It is clear that the prospects for individual Scots and the Scottish economy depend crucially on the quality of skills. So, where does Scotland stand?

Starting with the performance of Scots in school, Table 2 compares the attainments of pupils in a number of developed countries in maths and science. While there may be debate about the validity of surveys and the extent to which meaningful comparisons can be made between countries, the clear and depressing conclusion is that children in Scottish schools trail significantly behind their peers overseas, at least in maths and science. In both, our children are in the bottom half of the developed country league in grade 4. By grade 8, we have slipped further – relegation beckons. That England fares worse is little consolation. The reputation of Scotland for a 'guid education' may now be as accurate a portrayal of reality as *Oor Wullie* and *The Broons*.

Maths class: how we compare

Table 2 – performance in 4th and 8th grades compared with international averages, 1995			
Mathematics			
Country	Fourth grade Mean score	Country	Eighth grade Mean score
Korea	611	Korea	607
Japan	597	Japan	605
Netherlands*	577	Czech Republic	564
Czech Republic	567	Netherlands*	541
Austria*	559	Austria*	539
Ireland	550	Hungary	537
Hungary*	548	Australia*	530
Australia*	546	Ireland	527
United States	545	Canada	527
Canada	532	New Zealand	508
Scotland	520	England**	506
England**	513	Norway	503
Norway	502	United States**	500
New Zealand	499	Scotland*	498
Greece	492	Iceland	487
Portugal	475	Greece*	484
Iceland	474	Portugal	454
Science			
Country	Fourth grade Mean score	Country	Eighth grade Mean score
Korea	597	Czech Republic	574
Japan	574	Japan	571
United States	565	Korea	565
Austria*	565	Netherlands*	560
Australia*	562	Austria*	558
Netherlands*	557	Hungary	554
Czech Republic	557	England**	552
England**	551	Australia*	545
Canada	549	Ireland	538
Ireland	539	United States**	534
Scotland	536	Canada	531
Hungary*	532	Norway	527
New Zealand	531	New Zealand	526
Norway	530	Scotland**	517
Iceland	505	Greece*	497
Greece	497	Iceland	494
Portugal	480	Portugal	480

■ Sig higher than international average ■ Not sig different from international average ■ Sig lower than international average

The data in Table 2 are based on International Association for the Evaluation of Educational Achievement (IEA) surveys. IEA sets four criteria for samples in each country. Countries with no asterisk met all criteria in full. Countries marked * met all the criteria in part. Countries marked ** did not meet the criteria.

Source: IEA, in Education at a Glance, OECD 1997

One way of measuring skill attainment is looking at formal qualifications. Recognising the importance of education and training to Scotland's economic prospects, the Advisory Scottish Council for Education and Training Targets (ASCETT) set five targets for 2000. Four are expressed in terms of Scottish Vocational Qualifications (SVQs). There are five levels of SVQs and they allow different types of qualification to be compared on a consistent basis.

Chart 6 measures Scotland's progress towards some of the targets and compares Scotland with the UK. Target 1 focuses on fairly basic skills: 85 per cent of 19 year olds should have reached SVQ Level II of five Standard Grades at levels 1-3. In summer 1998, 74 per cent of 19 year olds had achieved this and Scotland marginally out-performed the UK. However, meeting the target in 2000 may be difficult.

Target 3 refers to SVQ Level III qualifications, equivalent to three Higher passes. SVQ Level III covers important 'technician' level skills and would usually allow entry to higher education. Here, Scotland markedly and consistently exceeds the level of achievement in the UK. In-mid 1998, half of the Scottish workforce had reached SVQ Level III compared with 44 per cent across the UK. However, the target for 2000 of 60 per cent of the workforce at this level remains distant and progress towards it since 1995 has been limited.

SVQ Level IV is equivalent to a first university degree and includes professional and management qualifications. Again, Scotland's workforce has a slightly higher share (28 per cent) of people with SVQ Level IV than the UK (25 per cent). The objective of having 30 per cent of the workforce at this level by 2000 is in sight.

Chart 6 shows that on all measures of workforce skills, Scotland performs better than the UK average. As with school attainments, however, that does not warrant complacency. With the exception of SVQ Level IV, the targets for 2000 look unlikely to be achieved and, on some of them, progress has been slow. Given that the targets were set with Scotland's developed world peers in mind, this is a source of concern.

Training and targets

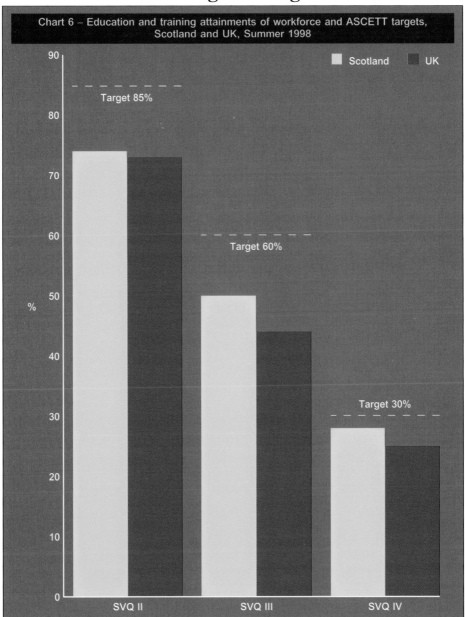

Chart 6 – Education and training attainments of workforce and ASCETT targets, Scotland and UK, Summer 1998

Source: Regional Competitiveness Indicators February 1999, Tables 8.1(a), (b)(i), (b)(ii), Government Statistical Service, DfEE

Notes:
1. The SVQ II target is expressed as a percentage of 19 year olds.
2. The SVQ III and IV targets are expressed as a percentage of the workforce.

113

Investors in People (IiP) is a UK-wide initiative which encourages employers to integrate training and development into the business planning process with the aim of boosting investment in skills. The final ASCETT target is that 70 per cent of organisations with more than 200 employees and 35 per cent employing more than 50 should gain IiP recognition by 2000. As Chart 7 shows, Scotland's performance here is very disappointing. In November 1998, only 24 per cent of larger employers had met the IiP standard, compared with 33 per cent across the UK. Among the smaller organisations the figure was a pitiful 13 per cent, compared with 18 per cent across the UK.

Some argue that IiP is no guarantee of an employer's commitment to training and development. However, the chart raises the wider issue of employer investment in training. For all the emphasis on public programmes, employers fund the bulk of vocational training in the UK. What is worrying is that Scottish employers may be investing less in training than those in the rest of the UK.

Chart 8 shows the proportion of employees and self-employed in Scotland and England in 1997 who had recently received job-related training. On most measures, there had been less training in Scotland than in England. Other data show that Scotland's share of employment-related training has been consistently lower than in the UK and there has been little change in the proportion of Scots being trained since the early 1990s. This pattern was repeated across most industries in 1996. Only in distribution, hotels and catering had a higher proportion of Scottish than UK employees received training.

A worrying picture is emerging. The importance of a skilled workforce is clear, but from school and into the labour market Scotland seems to be falling short of both international standards and the targets we have set ourselves. Moreover, although other parts of Britain fare worse in terms of skill attainment and school performance, Scottish employers appear to invest less in employee training and development.

Scotland appears to excel in one area of education and training. The share of the workforce with high level qualifications and the proportion

Workplace training: could do better

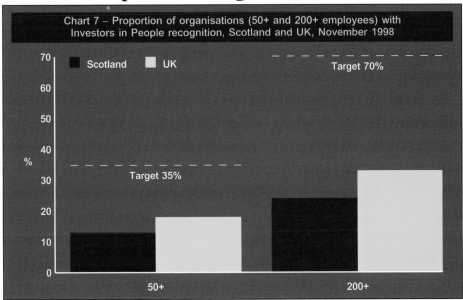

Source: Regional Competitiveness Indicators February 1999, Table 9, Government Statistical Service DfEE and IiP UK

Employers' contribution

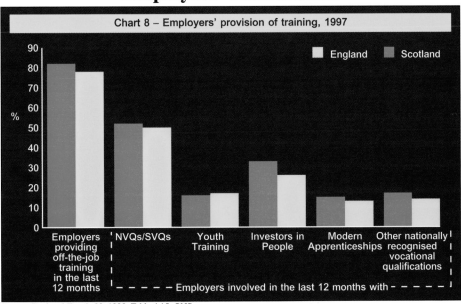

Source: Regional Trends 33, 1998, Table 4.15, ONS

of young people entering higher education are greater than in the rest of the UK. Chart 6 showed the proportion of Scots with SVQ Level IV attainment. Chart 9 illustrates the extent to which there is greater participation in higher education in Scotland. In part, that is a testament to the strength of the Scottish system. It also reflects the commitment of the current and previous governments to boosting higher education and providing the resources to allow the sector to expand.

It can only be a strength for Scotland to have a high and rising number of people in the workforce with graduate-level skill and this should feed through in time to productivity levels. The evidence shows that throughout the 1990s the proportion of Scottish domiciled graduates finding work in Scotland has risen. However, as successive UK governments have found, funding a growing higher education sector is costly. Given the inevitable budget constraints facing any government, this analysis suggests tough choices ahead for Scotland's Parliament.

In Chapter 10 we argue that one of the potential gains of devolution is that it will allow new approaches to be taken to policy making. In particular, it will be possible to use 'non-economic' powers – like education – to achieve economic goals. If the Parliament decides that higher living standards are one of its aims, that implies a need to raise productivity levels. Given Scotland's skill attainment performance, an early priority will be investment in schools and vocational education and training. This is essential if the gap between Scottish pupils and their international peers is to be bridged and if Scotland is to attain most of its self-imposed education and training targets.

One option is to shift the balance of resources within the education and training budget towards schools and 'lower level' vocational training – but this could imply fewer resources for higher education.

Meeting the skills challenge

For individual Scots and for the economy as a whole, enhancing skills is imperative. First, it is one of the few 'laws' of economics that improved living standards depend on higher productivity. Second, the jobs for which there is a growing need generally demand superior skills to those jobs which are disappearing. Third, if there are concerns about the extent of long-term unemployment, this chapter has demonstrated that one of the quickest routes to a job is acquiring skills. Finally, there is enough evidence to suggest that Scotland has weaknesses from classroom to shop, office and factory in developing the skills of its people.

The Parliament has the powers and resources to make a significant difference in this area. But the choices will not be easy and the solutions will not necessarily be found in higher spending. A debate is needed about the balance of spending between the various levels of education and training and how they should be funded. What should not be in dispute is the need to meet the skills challenge.

Higher education

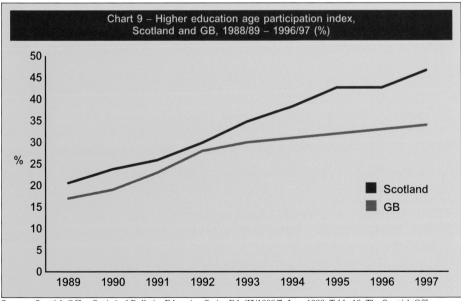

Chart 9 – Higher education age participation index, Scotland and GB, 1988/89 – 1996/97 (%)

Sources: Scottish Office Statistical Bulletin, Education Series Edn/J2/1998/7, June 1998, Table 10, The Scottish Office; SOED News Release 23, June 1998 (1295/98); Higher Education in the Learning Society, The National Committee of Inquiry into Higher Education, July 1997, Annexe G, Table 1

8

Key sectors of the Scottish economy

by Peter Wood

Why all sectors matter now

What are the ways in which Scotland, and the Scottish people, make their living? For many the title "Key sectors of the Scottish economy" conjures up visions of heavy engineering, 'metal bashing', whisky distilling and, for the more up to date, computer factories.

While all these have their place in the economy, the reality is that, as Chart 1 shows, most Scots earn their living by providing services rather than making things. Indeed, one sector – financial and business services – produces almost as much income, and employs almost as many people, as all of manufacturing industry. In the period 1991-1993, the output of the financial and business services sector in Scotland exceeded that of manufacturing, though this position has been reversed by quite rapid growth in manufacturing output in Scotland in more recent years.

What may also surprise many is that oil does not figure in the sources of Scottish income. This is because offshore oil production is not treated as 'Scottish' in official statistics (see Chapter 2).

Looking at where people work, rather than the value of output, tells broadly the same story. Chart 2 shows that manufacturing now employs barely three out every 20 Scottish workers, while services employ 15 out of 20. More than 8,000 are employed in making computers in Scotland, but almost twice as many are involved in providing services such as consultancy and maintenance connected with computer use. Manufacturing as a whole is still important in Scotland, accounting for one fifth of income and 15 per cent of jobs. But no individual manufacturing industry looms large in the Scottish economy.

Picking out key sectors of the economy runs the risk of implying that other sectors 'don't matter'. That would be wrong. An economy

Key sectors for Scotland

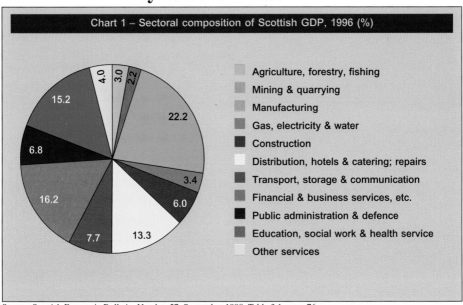

Source: Scottish Economic Bulletin, Number 57, September 1998, Table 3.1, page 76

Employment by sector

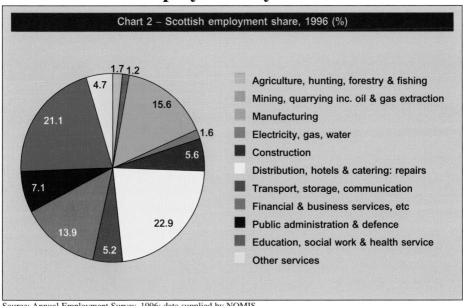

Source: Annual Employment Survey, 1996; data supplied by NOMIS

with a wide range of activities has important advantages in a rapidly changing world. One of the most important developments in Scotland has been the shift away from dependence on declining heavy industry.

What are the activities that will have greatest influence on the prosperity of Scotland in the next decade? Official statistics do not tell the whole story. They do not, for example, capture the full impact of onshore North Sea oil and gas which provides work and incomes across Scotland and demand for a wide range of Scottish-produced goods and services.

Restructuring and economic change

Scotland's image as a heavy industry economy was valid in the 1950s, but the last 25 years have seen radical changes. Chart 3 details the share of output accounted for by the main economic sectors in 1971. It can be compared with the data for 1996 in Chart 1.

While the share of output accounted for by some sectors – notably agriculture and public administration – has remained fairly stable, two have experienced major and contrary shifts. The manufacturing sector has seen its share of national output fall by a third, while the financial and business services sector has multiplied its share of the national output 'pie' more than threefold. As discussed above, manufacturing has recovered some ground recently. But long-term trends suggest that the financial and business services sector will once more overtake manufacturing.

Some of this shift is statistical. Over the years, many manufacturing companies have switched to buying in services previously provided within the firm, triggering a change in job classification. For example, when a manufacturing firm employs its own clerical workers to prepare the payroll, they are counted as being in the manufacturing sector. When the same firm decides to buy in this service from a firm of accountants, the workers who prepare the payroll will be counted in the service sector. But even allowing for this, it is clear there has been a massive switch in Scotland from making things to providing services.

The way we were

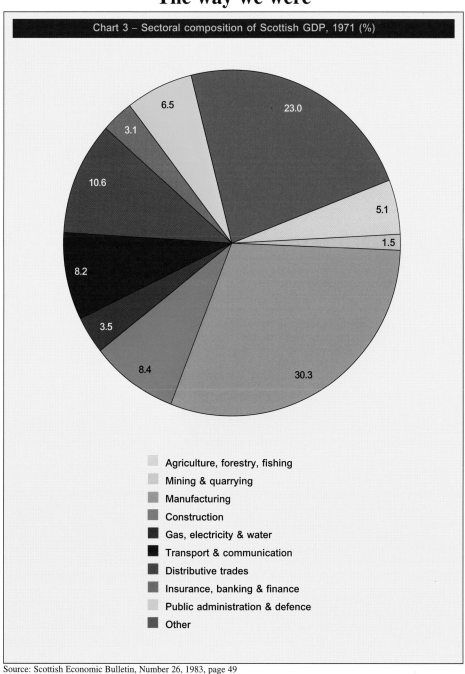

Chart 3 – Sectoral composition of Scottish GDP, 1971 (%)

- Agriculture, forestry, fishing
- Mining & quarrying
- Manufacturing
- Construction
- Gas, electricity & water
- Transport & communication
- Distributive trades
- Insurance, banking & finance
- Public administration & defence
- Other

Source: Scottish Economic Bulletin, Number 26, 1983, page 49

These changes have had profound effects on individuals and communities. The closure of steel plants, car factories and engineering works has consumed acres of newsprint – and been compared in popular song to the trauma of the Highland Clearances. This is really only half the score. It is hard to recall any ballads written about the opening of bank data processing centres or software companies.

One consequence of this change is that the economy in Scotland is now very similar to that of the rest of the UK, and rather more so than it is to the economies of some other developed countries of similar size. Chart 4 compares Scotland's economy with that of the UK and a number of other countries. Scotland, like the UK as a whole, has a small manufacturing sector and a large financial and business services sector. It is thus hardly surprising that Scotland's economy has converged with that of the UK. It has been part of the same market for hundreds of years while the factors that once made it distinctive – such as large-scale coal deposits – have lost their economic importance (Jeremy Peat and Stephen Boyle discuss the key differences that remain in Chapter 2).

Made in Scotland

Where Scottish manufacturing once meant steel and ships and heavy machines it now means food and drink, textiles and clothing and, above all, electronics. These three sectors provide half the manufacturing jobs in Scotland and more than half of all manufactured product output. However, the three sectors have little in common.

Electronics is the success story of Scottish manufacturing. Electronics manufacturing is diverse, but there are two main product groups: personal computers or workstations, and semiconductors. More than half the value of Scottish manufactured exports is accounted for by electronics products.

Output in the electronics sector has grown rapidly in the 1990s and with it employment. But there have been big increases in productivity, too.

Output: how Scotland compares

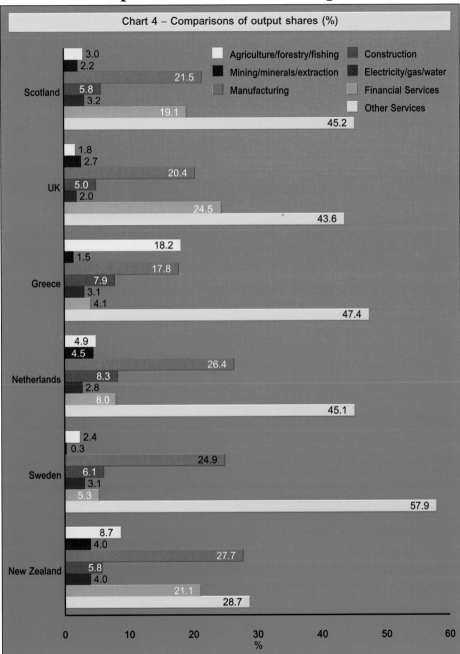

Chart 4 – Comparisons of output shares (%)

Legend:
- Agriculture/forestry/fishing
- Mining/minerals/extraction
- Manufacturing
- Construction
- Electricity/gas/water
- Financial Services
- Other Services

Scotland
- 3.0
- 2.2
- 21.5
- 5.8
- 3.2
- 19.1
- 45.2

UK
- 1.8
- 2.7
- 20.4
- 5.0
- 2.0
- 24.5
- 43.6

Greece
- 18.2
- 1.5
- 17.8
- 7.9
- 3.1
- 4.1
- 47.4

Netherlands
- 4.9
- 4.5
- 26.4
- 8.3
- 2.8
- 8.0
- 45.1

Sweden
- 2.4
- 0.3
- 24.9
- 6.1
- 3.1
- 5.3
- 57.9

New Zealand
- 8.7
- 4.0
- 27.7
- 5.8
- 4.0
- 21.1
- 28.7

%

Sources: Scottish Economic Bulletin Number 57 September 1998, Table 3.1; Datastream, OECD

In the 1990s the output of the Scottish manufacturing sector has held up well by comparison with the rest of the UK. Since 1990, the value of the output of Scottish manufacturing has grown by almost a third, while the UK's manufacturing sector has managed a mere 4 per cent growth. This performance is enough to stir any economic Braveheart. But as Charts 5 and 6 show, the electronics sector is the key. Indeed, if electronics is excluded, Scottish manufacturing output would have fallen over this period and would have lagged even the modest performance of the UK overall.

The factories of foreign-owned companies investing in the light of global market conditions dominate the sector. Markets for personal computers and semi-conductors are highly competitive. Scotland's success in attracting this investment is all the more outstanding as it has been achieved in the face of closures and job cutbacks by these companies elsewhere. Scotland has stayed ahead in one of the fastest and most dynamic games in the world economy. The challenge is to stay ahead and to ensure that this sector is embedded in Scotland.

If the electronics industry operates in a global market, the food and drink industry (with the important exception of whisky) services the UK market. Whisky production employs just one in five of the total in food and drink production, but produces more than 80 per cent of Scottish food and drink exports. Scotch whisky shares with electronics a high degree of foreign ownership and participation in a dynamic global market. But it enjoys the vital advantage that it cannot be legally manufactured outside Scotland.

Textiles and clothing is the manufacturing sector with arguably the greatest problems. Relatively high value products, such as knitwear, compete in dynamic international fashion markets; while the garment sector is exposed to intensifying competition from low-cost producers. Output in the sector fell by 9 per cent between 1990 and 1996.

The difference electronics makes

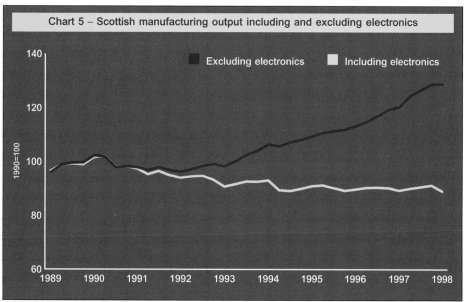

Source: Scottish Office Education & Industry Department, Index of Industrial Production & Construction

Not so sparky

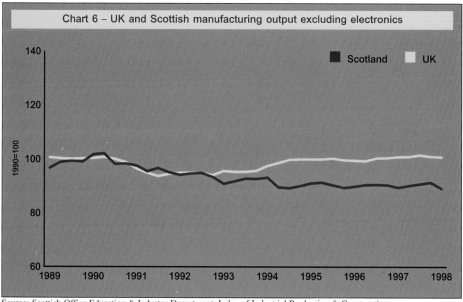

Source: Scottish Office Education & Industry Department, Index of Industrial Production & Construction

125

The impact of offshore oil and gas

North Sea oil, if not the most important element in the Scottish economy, has a high public profile and is the most sensitive in political terms. It is now more than 25 years since BP found oil in the North Sea and more than 20 years since production began of what was hailed – with some exaggeration – as the saviour of the UK.

Production now flows from more than 80 oil and 60 gas fields. While offshore oil and gas production is not included in Scottish output figures but placed in its own special category, employment in the sector is – both offshore and onshore – available from Scottish Office statistics.

More than 60,000 are employed in Scotland in North Sea oil and gas related activities. Chart 7 shows that most are employed in firms which do not form part of the oil and gas sector.

Some 6,000 are employed, onshore and offshore, in exploring for and producing oil and gas. A further 14,000 are employed in directly associated services – moving supplies to oil platforms, maintenance and other specialised services. The remaining 50,000 are employed in related activities including manufacturing and services, and in companies which depend mainly upon sales to the oil and gas sector. Most of these jobs are located in and around Aberdeen, making the north east of Scotland the most prosperous UK region outside the south east of England.

Oil and gas production is likely to continue for many years and is still rising. The oil price, in real terms (see Chart 8), is now far below the levels once thought uneconomic in difficult North Sea conditions. But production costs have also sunk – literally as well as financially – while the oil companies and their major contractors have achieved greater efficiencies. A notable feature of the sector in recent years has been the development of long-term contractual partnerships between the oil companies and their major service contractors. The aim has been to keep production economic by driving down costs.

The jobs that oil has brought

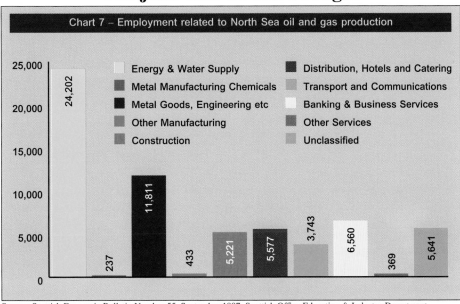

Source: Scottish Economic Bulletin Number 55, September 1997, Scottish Office Education & Industry Department

The oil price drama

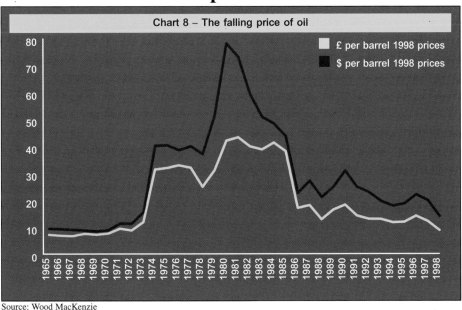

Source: Wood MacKenzie

Although production in the North Sea will continue for many years, much new UK production will come from the deeper and more dangerous waters of the North Atlantic west of Shetland. Production here depends upon new sub-sea technologies. But the pace of development is unpredictable given the perennially uncertain oil price outlook, lack of detailed knowledge on the amount of oil and environmental concerns.

Scotland's financial and investment portfolio

Financial and business services employ more than 250,000. Chart 9 shows that between 1984 and 1994 this sector created more new jobs than the total employed in electronics or in North Sea oil related activities. The strength of this sector is one of the distinctive features of the Scottish economy, although employment has fallen back from the 1995 peak.

The name of the sector gives the impression that it consists mainly of banks and insurance companies. But Chart 10 shows that only about one third of the jobs in the sector are in these categories, with the bulk accounted for by legal and computer services, accountancy, property services and industrial cleaning. Employment grew at about the same rate in finance as in other parts of the sector over the 1985-95 period. However, the most rapid growth has been in computer-related services, where employment leapt by 78 per cent between 1991 and 1996.

Although this sector is important for the UK as well as Scotland, the distinctive Scottish feature is the strong presence of banking, life assurance and fund management. A simple comparison of Scottish employment with UK figures indicates that the financial sector provides about the same share of employment in Scotland as in the whole of the UK. But this hides the fact that, Scotland, and particularly Edinburgh, is the main centre outside London for sophisticated financial services such as fund management.

Jobs surge in finance and banking

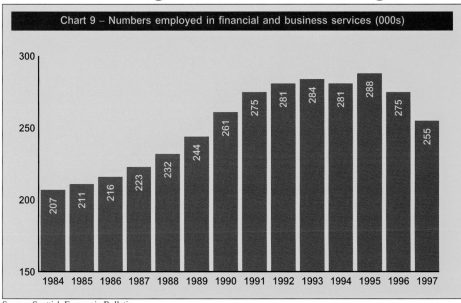

Source: Scottish Economic Bulletin

Where the jobs are

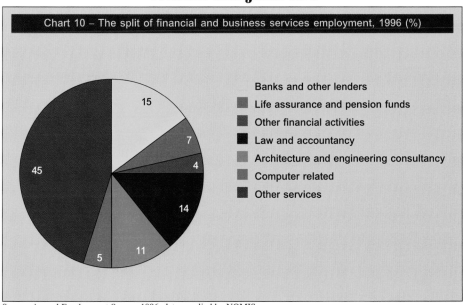

Source: Annual Employment Survey, 1996, data supplied by NOMIS

The rapid growth of investments managed by Scottish fund managers and insurance companies is shown in Chart 11. This expansion helped fuel the growth of employment of one quarter in Scottish financial companies between 1985 and 1995. Whether this growth pace will be sustained with the popularity of index tracker funds is moot.

Financial and business services employ about one in ten in Scotland and provided almost half of the new jobs created in the economy between 1985 and 1997. The sector's continued health is, therefore, vital to Scottish economic prospects. The reversal of employment growth after 1995, which also occurred at the UK level, indicates that the sector is not invulnerable.

Scottish fund managers face strong competition from larger London-based and international groups. The other Scottish financial institutions, although large in Scottish terms, are relatively small players in markets that are becoming ever more global.

Although business services employment will tend to rise for reasons related to technology and the changing ways in which businesses are organised, financial services would only be able to continue to grow if Scottish companies are innovative and competitive. The days of rapid employment growth have gone, while take-overs and pressures arising from the advent of the single European bourse present searching questions for the future of independent companies in Scotland's financial sector.

Mony a meikle...

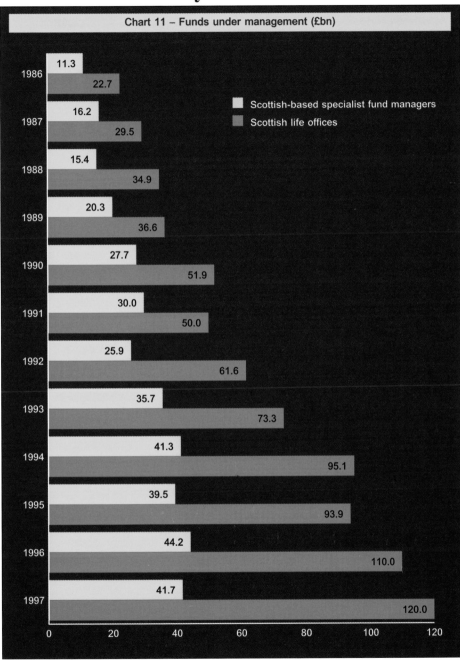

Chart 11 – Funds under management (£bn)

Scottish-based specialist fund managers
Scottish life offices

Source: Scottish Financial Enterprise

Scotland at the check-out

Retailing employs more than 200,000 in Scotland and has been an important job creator. Employment here grew by 8 per cent over the first half of the 1980s. About one in ten Scottish jobs are now in shops – almost exactly the same proportion as in the UK as a whole. Chart 12 shows how retail employment has special characteristics. Women fill almost seven out of ten jobs and six out of ten are part-time. These characteristics are sometimes held up as weaknesses. But for many workers, part-time employment best suits their personal circumstances.

Retailing boomed with the rest of the economy in the second half of the 1980s. Real (after inflation) income per person – the amount people have available to spend after tax – rose by 60 per cent between 1985 and 1990. Retail sales rose in line. This growth in incomes continued, at a slower rate, in the 1990s.

Income growth has enabled retail employment to rise, but other changes have been unfolding. Despite sharply higher spending by consumers, there are now fewer shops in Scotland today than there were 20 years ago. Grocery superstores have replaced local or high street food shops. In 1975 there was a handful of superstores in Scotland. Today there are nearly 100. Some, though not all, of the superstores are located in shopping centres on the edge of towns or cities. Few are located in 'traditional' town centres. The last decade has also seen the emergence of retail parks for non-food products such as electrical goods, furniture, shoes and sportswear. Before the mid-1980s these developments were almost unknown in Scotland. Now there are around 30 parks on the edge or outer areas of towns, reflecting, inter alia, wider car use.

These developments have sparked concern about the future of the town centre and their feared decline into desertion and dereliction. But the larger town centres appear to be faring well. Accessible by public transport, and offering a wide range of goods, they continue to attract shoppers. The main losers in the process of change appear to be the suburban shopping centres that are neither in the centre nor on the edge of town. Many, though not all, such areas are falling into decline as shoppers move to out of town or edge of town superstores for food shopping and to the town centre for higher value goods.

UK chains, especially food retailing, increasingly dominate retailing. Although there are more than 22,000 shops in Scotland, £3 out of every £10 are spent in the shops of just five large groups. Most food in Scotland is sold through five major retail chains, and Tesco took over the last surviving Scottish-based supermarket business a few years ago. It appears to be harder for smaller operators to survive in food retailing and very difficult for any new food retailer to break into the market on a large scale.

Environmental and transport concerns are likely to figure prominently in retail development policy. Attempts to discourage car use by higher taxation may affect new out of town retail developments. But they are unlikely to impact on the consumers' endorsement of existing ones while adding both to business and consumer costs.

At the check-out

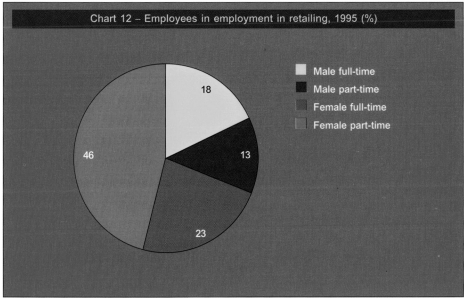

Chart 12 – Employees in employment in retailing, 1995 (%)

- Male full-time
- Male part-time
- Female full-time
- Female part-time

Source: Census of Employment, 1995, data supplied by NOMIS

Good environmental intentions may have other adverse effects. The prevention of new development in locations which can compete with existing centres will make it harder for new competitors to enter the retail market. Rising incomes will continue to drive up spending to the particular benefit of those retailers who occupy the best trading locations – their favoured position protected by the planning system. The 1998 McKinsey report on UK productivity performance laid strong emphasis on how planning laws were damaging competitiveness.

The tourist also spends

Tourism is an important part of the Scottish economy, though there is no tourism 'industry' in the official statistics. Spending by tourists is estimated at more than £2 billion a year.

The nearest match to tourism is the hotels and catering sector. But many businesses in this sector depend on the custom of locals rather than of those who are travelling for pleasure or business. Meanwhile, those in other sectors such as retailing earn part of their living from tourism.

More than 130,000 work in the hotels and catering sector. Like retailing, it is characterised by a high proportion of female employment and part-time working. The key features are shown in Chart 13. What the figures do not show is that much of the employment, especially in hotels in rural areas, is seasonal, with people being laid off in winter.

In line with Scotland's status as a tourist destination, hotels and catering employ a greater share of the workforce than is the case elsewhere in the UK. The sector provides about one in every 15 Scottish jobs, compared with one in every 18 in the UK as a whole.

Employment in this sector has been virtually static over the last five years. This reflects the absence of any sustained growth in the tourism sector and tourism activity. While tourism is growing globally, overseas visits to Scotland are influenced by the exchange rate and tend to fall when the pound is strong. Scotland's main tourism market is, in fact,

England and Scotland competes with a range of other destinations for the English tourism pound. In recent years the strength of the pound has encouraged UK tourist visits to the continent.

The main challenges to the industry are to raise quality standards in order to retain market share and to develop 'out of season' tourism. This both spreads demand across the year and capitalises on the growing trend to take two or even three short break holidays each year.

Built in Scotland

Construction – from roads to house building – provides about 6 per cent of Scottish income and about the same proportion of Scottish employment. This proportion has fallen slowly over the last 20 years as other sectors of the economy have grown more quickly.

Looking after the tourist

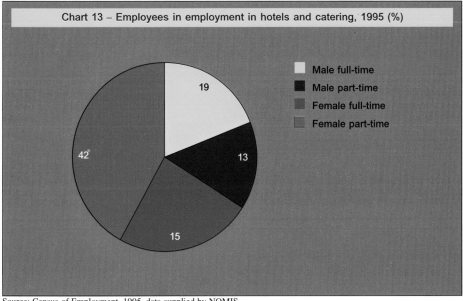

Chart 13 – Employees in employment in hotels and catering, 1995 (%)

Male full-time
Male part-time
Female full-time
Female part-time

19

13

42°

15

Source: Census of Employment, 1995, data supplied by NOMIS

The construction sector ranges from large civil engineering groups building motorways, office blocks and other major projects, to small local building firms specialising in repair work. As many as one third of the people working in the sector are self-employed, i.e. one-person firms.

Chart 14 shows that the largest single type of work – accounting for just under half of output – is repair and maintenance. House building is the second largest category, followed by infrastructure – roads, sewers, water mains, etc.

Repair work and house building provide a stable market. Indeed house building has been on an upward trend in recent years. But certain types of public investment – such as roads – look set to fall.

Large construction companies are most exposed to cuts in such items as the road programme. Large-scale construction work, especially civil engineering, is closely related to government spending. This is why construction companies have become involved in finance as the government has sought to use private money raised through the Private Finance Initiative to pay for public investment. They have thus had to bring forward not only project plans but, in partnership with financial institutions, proposals for financing and operating such infrastructure.

Government: Scotland's biggest employer

Scotland's biggest employer of all is government – local and national. One Scottish worker in four – more than 500,000 in total – works for government in one way or another. Of this total, about half are in health or social work, more than one third are in education and the balance in miscellaneous administrative and service functions.

Despite continual stories over the last two decades concerning public spending 'cuts' and inadequacies, the share of national output accounted for by education, health and social work has risen – in Scotland as in the UK – by more than one third. Chart 15 also shows that the share of output given over to public administration has fallen slowly but steadily over that period, reflecting privatisation and contracting out.

136

Building blocks

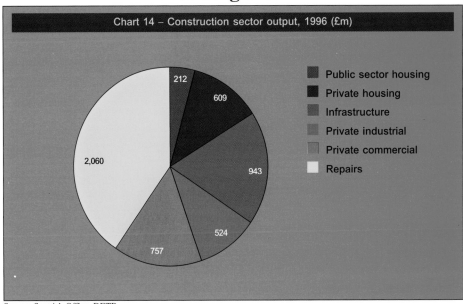

Source: Scottish Office, DETR

Scotland's bigger state

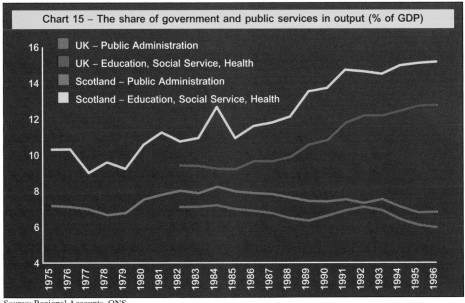

Source: Regional Accounts, ONS

Public spending in Scotland is, relative to population, higher than in England and Wales. For example, a study conducted of local authority spending in 1993/94 demonstrated that local government spending on services per person was 18 per cent higher in Scotland than in England.

Similarly, the Scottish Office's figures indicate that central government spending per person is about 25 per cent higher in Scotland than in the rest of the UK.

This spending difference shows up in various ways. Scottish schools tend to have smaller class sizes than schools in England and a lower ratio of pupils to teachers. Whether this extra spending produces better educational results is debatable. There is some evidence that at the Standard Grade/GCSE stage Scottish pupils do better. But this difference is not there if we compare the levels of achievement, in terms of the proportion of pupils obtaining the usual minimum number of A levels/Highers needed to enter university.

Higher central government spending is particularly noticeable in health and social services. Scotland has about 8 per cent of the UK's population and 9 per cent of employment, but it has 11 per cent of the UK's health and social services employees. Studies of service delivery do suggest that Scottish residents benefit from this extra spending in terms of shorter waiting times at accident and emergency departments.

Conclusion

Scotland's economy has, over time, come to resemble more closely that of the rest of the UK. Features that still make Scotland distinctive within the UK include:

- a manufacturing sector increasingly dependent on the performance of foreign-owned electronics firms;
- the contribution of North Sea oil and gas activity;
- a strong and locally controlled financial services sector;
- a large and relatively well-funded public sector.

9

Financing Scottish government
by Gavin McCrone

The whole issue of financing Government in Scotland is contentious and complex but crucial. This book goes to press just ahead of the first sitting of the Scottish Parliament. Even at this late date, confusion continues in the public mind, and probably in the minds of the many politicians who expect to take part, over how Scotland's public finances will work. Hence the importance of a full, accurate and accessible discussion of the present position and the prospects. The White Paper says that "Scotland will continue to benefit from an appropriate share of United Kingdom public expenditure" and that the present block arrangement will remain in place adjusted annually by the Barnett formula.[1] This is usually taken to mean that expenditure will continue to be based on need. But how does the formula work and has it resulted in a provision of expenditure based on need? Will it do so in the future? Few people could produce creditable answers to these questions.

Some people have argued that, rather than be dependent on Westminster for a share of the UK's public expenditure, Scotland should simply fund its expenditure from its own tax revenue, whether it remains within the UK or becomes independent.[2] But how many people understand what that implies? Are there presently net fiscal transfers to Scotland from the rest of the United Kingdom or vice versa? The Scottish Office has published figures which might have been expected to settle this latter issue, but they have been subjected to attack and the resulting controversy has left many people as confused as ever. Yet the success of devolution will be heavily dependent on financial arrangements that are seen to be flexible and fair, not only to Scotland but to other parts of the UK.

The proposals

The essence of the proposed scheme is that existing arrangements that apply to Scottish Office expenditure under the Secretary of State would continue with only slight modification after devolution. With a few exceptions (the most

1. Scottish Office (1997), *Scotland's Parliament*, Cm 3658, Edinburgh: HMSO.
2. This line has been frequently argued in *The Scotsman* newspaper as well, of course, by the SNP.

important of which is spending on agriculture) Scottish Office expenditure is treated as a block, within which the Secretary of State is free to decide his own spending priorities. Annual changes to the block, whether increases or decreases, are determined by what has come to be known as the 'Barnett formula', after the Chief Secretary to the Treasury in 1979, at the time of the previous Labour Government's proposals for devolution. This formula only applies to changes, not to existing expenditure inherited from past decisions which is carried forward each year.

The formula is intended to be based on the ratio of Scotland's population to that of England and is not related either to income levels or to need. But the ratio of Scotland's actual population to that of England has gradually declined over the last 20 years from 11.1 per cent in 1979 to 10.4 per cent in 1997.[3] When the Barnett formula was introduced in 1979 it was based on a ratio of 10/85 (11.79 per cent) which turned out to be an overestimate of Scotland's population ratio even at the time. Nevertheless, it remained unchanged until 1992 when it was adjusted to 10.66 per cent – the so-called 'Portillo recalibration'. This ratio has continued since.

Scotland has therefore benefited from a ratio for allocating public expenditure changes, supposedly based on population, which has tended to be out of date. The White Paper, however, makes it explicit that the Barnett formula is intended to be a population based ratio, and says that for the future 'the formula will be updated from time to time to take account of population and other technical changes'.[4]

Subsequently, in response to pressure from English MPs, Alastair Darling as Chief Secretary told the Treasury Select Committee that it would be revised annually.[5]

Total expenditure in 1996/97 for which the Scottish Office was responsible amounted to £14.9 billion, of which the block comprised £13.8 billion and agriculture, fisheries and food £600 million.[6] It is to this £13.8 billion, therefore, that the formula at present applies; expenditure on

3. CSO (annual), *Annual Abstract of Statistics*, London: HMSO
4. Scottish Office, op. cit. p. 22 paras 7.6 and 7.7.
5. Reported in *The Scotsman*, 15 December 1997.
6. Scottish Office and HM Treasury (1998), *Serving Scotland's Needs: The Government's Expenditure Plans*, Cm 3914, London: HMSO, p. 13.

agriculture is largely determined by Europe-wide decisions on the Common Agricultural Policy.

The Scottish Parliament will inherit these arrangements with little change. There will be a new Scottish block to take account of some small changes in responsibility for functions, but it will not differ substantially from its predecessor. Scottish Office expenditure, however, even taking block and non-block together, is well short of the total for identifiable public expenditure in Scotland, which amounted to £24.7 billion in 1996/97.[7] The largest part of the difference is accounted for by £9.1 billion social security expenditure; this is not a Scottish Office responsibility and not a service to be devolved. Chart 1 shows the breakdown by programme of Scottish identifiable public expenditure in 1996/97.

The Scottish Parliament will, however, have a tax varying power that was not available to Secretaries of State. This amounts to 3p in the pound, either up or down, on the basic rate of income tax set by the UK Parliament. This power does not apply to lower or higher rates of income tax, nor does it apply to savings or

7. Scottish Office (1998), *Government Expenditure and Revenue in Scotland 1996/97*, Glasgow, p. 9.

Where the money goes

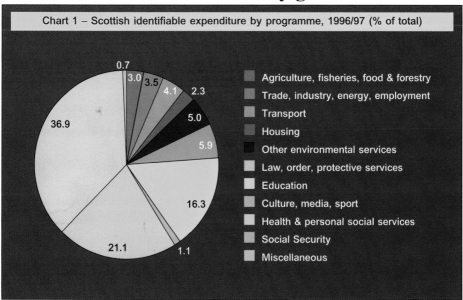

Chart 1 – Scottish identifiable expenditure by programme, 1996/97 (% of total)

- Agriculture, fisheries, food & forestry
- Trade, industry, energy, employment
- Transport
- Housing
- Other environmental services
- Law, order, protective services
- Education
- Culture, media, sport
- Health & personal social services
- Social Security
- Miscellaneous

Source: Government Expenditure and Revenue in Scotland 1996/97, Table 4, The Scottish Office

dividend income. The 1999 Budget, by removing the 20 per cent tax band and introducing a 10 per cent band for a more restricted range of income, has widened the scope of the basic rate. In consequence, the yield of a 1p variation is now £230 million (as compared with £140 million at the time of the White Paper) and full use of the power would yield £690 million.[8] But at its maximum this still amounts to just under 5 per cent of expenditure on the block.

The Scottish Parliament will be responsible for local government in Scotland, and an indirect way in which further finance might be raised could be to restrict grant allocations to local authorities, thereby pushing them to raise the council tax. But revenue from the council tax only accounts for some 16 per cent of local authority expenditure, so that any restriction in government funding would have a disproportionate effect on the tax rate. An alternative might be to decouple the unified business rate from rates in England, thereby either giving the Scottish Parliament the power to set the rate or returning it to local authorities as used to be the case. However, this would be extremely unpopular with the business community who, especially in the commercial sector, felt that the old Scottish rates system penalised them in comparison with their counterparts in England. The consequence therefore might be significant damage to business and to employment, though this would of course depend on how the power was used.

Public expenditure in practice

The key characteristic of Scottish public expenditure is that for services where spending can be attributed to Scotland (identifiable public expenditure), the total amount spent per head is substantially above the UK average and higher still in comparison with England. Table 1 shows that in 1996/97 the level of spending per head was in aggregate 119 per cent of the UK average and 124 per cent of that in England. The difference has narrowed slightly since 1988/89 but not continuously. Its lowest point was in 1991/92; after that it rose slowly but has fallen again in the latest year. Chart 2 shows the latest available figures for identifiable public expenditure per head in England, Wales and Northern Ireland, as well as in Scotland.

8. HM Treasury (1999), *Financial Statement and Budget Report*, London: HMSO.

Spending more in Scotland

Table 1 – Scottish identifiable public expenditure per head		
	UK=100	**England=100**
1986/87	122	128
1987/88	124	130
1988/89	123	130
1989/90	119	124
1990/91	118	123
1991/92	114	118
1992/93	118	123
1993/94	119	124
1994/95	120	125
1995/96	120	125
1996/97	119	124

Note: Because of differences in definition, figures for the first three years are not exactly comparable with other years and may be 1 or 2 per cent too high

Source: Government Expenditure amd Revenue in Scotland 1986/87 – 1996/97 editions, Table 2 A/B, The Scottish Office

How spending per head compares

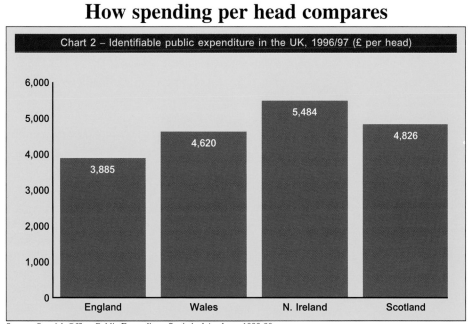

Chart 2 – Identifiable public expenditure in the UK, 1996/97 (£ per head)

Source: Scottish Office, Public Expenditure Statistical Analyses 1998-99

Chart 3 shows that Scottish spending is above UK levels per head for all major services. The difference is very small in law and order and in culture, media and sport. It is largest, not surprisingly, in agriculture, fisheries and food and in housing (because of the larger social rented sector). In health and education, the two biggest programmes, it is 19 per cent and 26 per cent above UK levels respectively.

This situation prompts two questions. First, why is Scottish public expenditure per head so much higher than in England, and second, why has the gap not narrowed if, under the Barnett formula, Scotland has, at least for that part of public expenditure that comprises the block, been getting only its population share of any United Kingdom increases in expenditure?

There are, of course, different public expenditure needs in Scotland from those in England, and it has been a key principle of the UK public expenditure system that spending is in accordance with need, without regard either to revenue raised in a particular area or any strict population share. It is not difficult to think of features of Scotland that justify higher levels of expenditure: the large land area and consequent geographical sparsity of population affect a wide range of services – class size in education, doctors' lists, miles of road to maintain, cost of housing etc; Scotland's poor health record (notably one of the highest incidences of heart disease in Western Europe and a high incidence of cancer, especially in the west of Scotland); four major medical schools and associated hospitals training doctors for the UK as a whole and well beyond Scotland's own needs; a large number of students from south of the border at Scottish universities so that the number of university places is well in excess of the needs of Scottish school leavers. But it is impossible to say how far these special factors justify the actual difference between Scottish and English levels of expenditure.

A study to assess needs was carried out in 1978 preparatory to the scheme of devolution set out in the Scotland Act of that year. It found that special factors justified a level of spending per head in Scotland, 16 per cent above that in England on the services then proposed for devolution, which were more restricted than the present Scottish block.[9]

9. HM Treasury (1979), *Needs Assessment Study: A Report*, London, especially pp. 5 and 27-28.

Sector spending compared

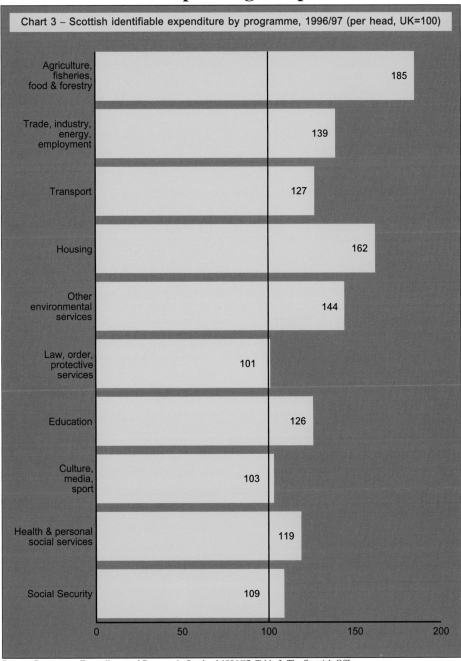

Chart 3 – Scottish identifiable expenditure by programme, 1996/97 (per head, UK=100)

Agriculture, fisheries, food & forestry	185
Trade, industry, energy, employment	139
Transport	127
Housing	162
Other environmental services	144
Law, order, protective services	101
Education	126
Culture, media, sport	103
Health & personal social services	119
Social Security	109

Source: Government Expenditure and Revenue in Scotland 1996/97, Table 3, The Scottish Office

This compared with an actual level of spending that was 22 per cent above England per head in 1976/77. This kind of exercise is of course fraught with difficulty – subjective judgements have to be made – and it is possible to have reservations about such work, some of which the study itself set out. Moreover, the study is 20 years old. But even allowing for all this, there appear to be no obvious reasons to justify a larger differential now.

A possible reason for the failure of the Barnett formula to produce more marked convergence is that it only applies to the block, not to identifiable expenditure as a whole. Since the block is only 56 per cent of identifiable expenditure, convergence in block services could be concealed by an increasing disparity in the remainder. Unfortunately it is not easy to compare expenditure on the block with equivalent services in England, since the figures are not published. But Table 2 shows the effect on the comparison if the two largest non-block services, social security and agriculture, fisheries, food and forestry are removed. It is then clear that there has indeed been a more marked convergence in the remaining services than in identifiable services as a whole. The gap between spending per head in Scotland and England for these remaining services is larger, because social security is a very large programme and the difference there is quite small, but Scottish expenditure per head on the remainder has come down from about 40 per cent to 30 per cent above the English level (32 to 24 per cent above the UK average) over the ten-year period to 1996/97.

But if this shows that the Barnett formula is bringing about the expected convergence, the gap is still large. It is perhaps surprising, since it is a population based ratio, that it has not narrowed further and had a more obvious impact on identifiable expenditure as a whole. Among the possible explanations are the following:

• The Barnett formula, as explained above, was above the true population share when it was introduced in 1979 and became progressively more so until the 1992 Portillo recalibration; thereafter it got out of date again and only in the White Paper has it been proposed to adjust it to the population ratio regularly.

- The last 20 years have, with a few exceptions, been years of tight public expenditure restraint and fairly low inflation; clearly that gives the formula, which applies only to changes, little to bite on.
- Until 1985, the formula applied to real increases only, the Treasury otherwise rolling forward the figures from one year to another with an inbuilt allowance for inflation.
- And finally, the formula has occasionally been bypassed either because a pay award, for example in the health service, has been funded centrally, or because Secretaries of State have been successful in advocating exceptional treatment.

Whatever the reasons, the outlook for devolution is hardly reassuring. With a Barnett formula recalibrated regularly for changes in population, it is likely to bite much harder in the future; and with a Scottish administration that may sooner or later be of a different political complexion from the government at Westminster, the environment may be less favourable to the pleading of exceptional factors than in the past. Moreover, whereas past negotiations took place in confidence between Ministers in the same government, in future they

Core spending ratios still higher

Table 2 – Scottish identifiable public expenditure per head excluding social security		
	UK=100	**England=100**
1986/87	132	141
1987/88	139	142
1988/89	139	142
1989/90	129	137
1990/91	127	134
1991/92	119	125
1992/93	123	128
1993/94	126	132
1994/95	126	132
1995/96	127	133
1996/97	124	130

Source: Government Expenditure and Revenue in Scotland 1986/87 – 1996/97, The Scottish Office

are likely to be conducted much more publicly. Already public opinion in England is more aware than it has been hitherto that Scotland appears to get a favourable deal, and demands are beginning to be heard for the level of spending either to be justified or brought down to average UK levels.

This debate is likely to become increasingly raucous with strong pressure, especially from some English regions, for an overhaul of the system. Attention has usually centred on the Barnett formula as the reason for Scotland's higher level of funding, and obviously that is to misunderstand the formula. But it must be expected that exceptions to the strict application of Barnett will be more difficult to obtain.

Yet, from the Scottish point of view, it is important to understand what the strict application of Barnett means: if expenditure is increased in England, say, by 3 per cent, and that is just enough to cover inflation, the same per head increase in Scotland might be only 2 or 2.5 per cent on the higher Scottish base and therefore a cut in real terms. This so-called 'Barnett squeeze' is hardly a propitious basis on which to launch a major constitutional reform. The taxation power available to the Scottish Parliament, even if used, could not compensate for this squeeze; it is so modest that it could easily be exhausted in a couple of years.[10]

Scotland's fiscal balance

Faced with this situation there are those that argue, and not only the SNP, or in the context of full independence, that the best solution would be to give the Scottish Parliament much greater fiscal autonomy so that it funded its expenditure from Scottish tax revenue. This would certainly remove what is likely to become a major area of dispute between Holyrood and Westminster. While superficially attractive, however, this approach does not offer a solution. Indeed a move to self-financing would be likely to precipitate a more abrupt spending crisis than the gradual squeeze towards convergence produced by the strict application of the Barnett formula.

The figures set out in Table 3 are largely taken from Government Expenditure & Revenue in Scotland (GERS). They are the only official

10. The problems of the 'Barnett squeeze' are well set out in N. Kay (1998), *The Scottish Parliament and the Barnett Formula*, Fraser of Allander Quarterly Economic Commentary, Vol. 24, No. 1, pp. 32-49.

estimates, but figures have also been published by the SNP. Both sets of figures have been subjected to widespread criticism.[11]

Any attempt to produce a fiscal balance for Scotland has to rely on figures of varying quality, many of which are estimates. This is particularly true for revenue. On the expenditure side, the figures for identifiable expenditure are robust, but those for non-identifiable and much of what is categorised as 'other expenditure' less so. For most of these items an allocation can only be made to Scotland by making assumptions about an appropriate share of what is inherently an indivisible service. This is true of defence, foreign representation overseas and interest on the national debt. The assumptions used in GERS are to apply Scotland's population share to defence and foreign representation and the non-oil GDP share (which now differs very little from the population share) to interest on the national debt.

Scotland's revenue, excluding oil revenues, is now approximately equal to its share of the UK population at 8.7 per cent (see Table 3). Expenditure, on the

11. SNP (1996), *Scotland Pays Her Way*, Edinburgh. Rather surprisingly, although this publication also gives figures for 1996/97 it appeared two years before the official Scottish Office figures and before the publication of the Treasury's figures on identifiable expenditure for that year.

Scotland's balance sheet

Table 3 – Scotland's fiscal position, 1996/97					
Expenditure			**Revenue**		
	£bn	% of UK		£bn	% of UK
Identifiable	24.7	10.4	Income Tax	5.5	8.0
Scottish Office	14.9		Nat. Insurance cont.	4.2	9.0
Social Security	9.1		VAT	4.0	8.6
Non-identifiable	3.1	8.7	Local authority taxes	2.2	9.0
Defence	1.9	8.7	All other revenue	8.7	9.1
Other expenditure	4.0	9.7	Total	24.7	8.7
Debt Interest	2.5	9.2	(Deficit excl. oil & gas)	7.1	
Total	31.8	10.1	Oil & gas revenue	2.9	80.3
Privatisation	-0.4	8.6	Borrowing requirement	3.8	
			(as % of GDP)	5.8	
Total	31.4	10.1	**Total**	31.4	10.1

Sources: Government Expenditure and Revenue in Scotland 1996-97, The Scottish Office; Expenditure and Revenues for the UKCS, A. Kemp & L. Stephen, Aberdeen University

other hand, is 10.1 per cent of the UK total, well above the population share, principally because identifiable expenditure is 10.4 per cent. The result, before including revenue from the Continental Shelf and a share of UK privatisation receipts, is a substantial deficit amounting to £7.1 billion.

The picture is incomplete, however, without a share of oil and gas revenues, since these are of course part of UK public sector income, and so much of the oil is in fields off the Scottish coast. Chart 4 shows UK tax revenue from oil and gas since 1975/76. In the past, the SNP have based their estimates on a 90 per cent share of the revenue accruing to Scotland. Division of the North Sea is a complex matter and negotiations could turn out to be disputatious and lengthy. The Government in GERS is more cautious and shows the effect of including oil and gas revenues on various assumptions varying between 0 and 100 per cent.

Recently published research by Professor Alex Kemp of Aberdeen University, not available at the time of the last edition of GERS, has enabled this problem to be tackled with much greater confidence and authority.[12] He applies the international rules for division of offshore waters and has carefully analysed the financial circumstances of both oil and gas fields in the North Sea. He finds that the Scottish share depends not only on how the dividing line is drawn between England and Scotland, but also on the price of oil. Since much of the northern North Sea is very deep and the fields there are more expensive to develop, when the oil price falls the profit and tax revenue from these fields falls more than for the less costly fields in shallower water to the south. In the past, therefore, when the oil price was very high, the Scottish share of tax revenue was also very high, reaching a peak of 98 per cent in 1982; but with the much lower price now prevailing, not only are UK revenues much less than in the early 1980s, despite similar levels of production, but the Scottish share is also less. For 1996/97 the share was 80 per cent and, with the sharp fall in oil prices since then, it was estimated at 75 per cent for the calendar year 1997 and 66 per cent for 1998.

12. A. Kemp and L. Stephen (1999), *Expenditures In and Revenues From the UKCS: Estimating the Hypothetical Scottish Shares 1970-2000*, North Sea Oil Occasional Paper No. 70, University of Aberdeen: Department of Economics. The information in this publication was supplemented by a conversation with Professor Kemp.

To complete the fiscal balance for 1996/97, therefore, the appropriate Scottish share of revenue from oil and gas is £2.9 billion. This still leaves an overall borrowing requirement of £3.8 billion after taking account also of a share of UK privatisation receipts. To express this as a proportion of Scottish GDP, however, a similar share of GDP arising from the Continental Shelf should be added to the normal Scottish figure. This increases Scotland's GDP by £11.0 billion to £65.4 billion, against which the borrowing requirement amounts to 5.8 per cent. In 1996/97 the UK's borrowing requirement was 3.0 per cent of GDP and it has fallen since then to only 0.1 per cent in 1997/98. Under the rules established by the Maastricht Treaty for Economic and Monetary Union, 3 per cent is the maximum permitted deficit for members unless there are exceptional circumstances. It is clear therefore that, if Scotland had to live within its own resources, a deficit of 5.8 per cent, especially at a relatively favourable point of the economic cycle, would be unsustainable. To reduce it to 3 per cent, tax increases, public expenditure cuts or a combination of the two would be required, amounting to at least £1.8 billion.

Rise and fall of North Sea revenues

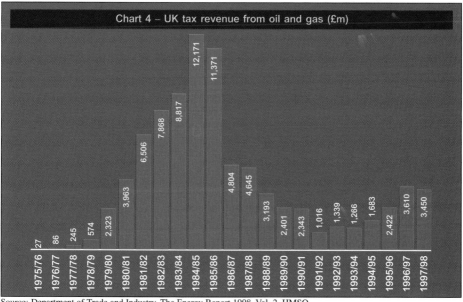

Source: Department of Trade and Industry, The Energy Report 1998, Vol. 2, HMSO

Before leaving this subject, it is necessary to refer to some of the criticisms that have been made of the GERS figures. The most detailed critique is that by Cuthbert and Cuthbert.[13] They make a lot of points but their most important criticisms concern the estimates of income tax revenue and the net contribution to the budget of the European Union. As Table 3 shows, income tax revenue in Scotland is estimated at £5.5 billion, 8.0 per cent of the UK total. This is based on a sample survey and is perhaps suspiciously low, given that Scotland has 8.7 per cent of the UK population and a GDP per head only marginally below the UK average in 1996.

But even if Scotland had its full GDP share of the UK revenue from income tax the difference would only be £440 million. Cuthbert and Cuthbert argue that the official figure is understated by £270 million. The Scottish Office estimate, however, is obtained from the Inland Revenue, and the low figure may not be unreasonable if full account is taken of the distribution of income in Scotland, which differs considerably from the UK, with significantly fewer taxpayers in the higher income bands.

On the contribution to the European Union the Cuthberts appear to have a valid point, but if one accepts it, one opens a can of worms. Under non-identifiable expenditure a figure is included for Scotland's share of the UK's net contribution based, according to the Cuthberts, on Scotland's share of non-oil GDP; they put this at £120 million. They argue that this is too high because Scotland receives a high share of the total payments made to the UK from both the Common Agricultural Policy and the Structural Funds, implying that Scotland's net contribution should be much less than the GDP share. But this would, of course, have repercussions. The United Kingdom receives, under the terms of the Fontainebleau agreement, a substantial rebate from the EU amounting to around £2 billion a year (£2.9 bn ECU in 1996).[14]

13. J. Cuthbert and M. Cuthbert (1998), *A Critique of GERS*, Fraser of Allander Quarterly Economic Commentary, Vol. 24, No. 1.
14. HM Treasury (1998), *Chancellor of the Exchequer's Departments: Public Expenditure*, Cm 3917, London: HMSO, pp. 128-138 and CEC (1998), *Financing the European Union: Commission Report on the Operation of the Own Resources System*, COM (1998) 560 final, Brussels.

This has the effect of reducing the UK's net contribution from about 0.5 to 0.2 per cent of GNP. But the continuation of this rebate is in doubt in future EU budget renegotiations, given that several other countries now have net contributions equal to or even exceeding, as a percentage of GNP, what the UK would pay without the rebate. If Scotland were a member of the EU in its own right, and particularly if it had a net contribution to the EU budget well below 0.5 per cent, the chances of it negotiating for itself a continuation of the Fontainebleau rebate must be considered negligible. Nor can maintenance of existing support received by Scotland from the Common Agricultural Policy and the Structural Funds be taken for granted. They are subject to renegotiation this year anyway and must take account of the EU's Agenda 2000. Furthermore, the demands to trim back existing levels of expenditure will be intensified if the budget is to cater for the much greater needs of applicant countries in central and eastern Europe.

Conclusion

Whatever constitutional arrangement was in prospect for Scotland there would be a budgetary problem. Even if the Secretary of State system were to continue, Scotland's higher level of identifiable public spending is now so well known in England that there would be pressure to reduce it, and the strict application of the Barnett formula would have the effect of bringing gradual but painful convergence.

Devolution simply makes the problem more explicit: negotiations which were previously done in private between Ministers in the same Government will henceforth be much more public. And if at some time the party in power at Westminster is different from that at Holyrood, the pressure to bring convergence could intensify. Making Scotland self-financing offers no solution; it would merely make the crisis more immediate, because the present level of deficit, even including oil and gas revenues, is too high to be sustainable.

Trying to find flaws in the statistics, as many commentators have done, does not seem to offer a way out. Scotland already contributes its population share of non-oil revenue and, with non-oil GDP slightly below the UK average per head, it is implausible to argue that it should be much higher. The 25 per cent of expenditure that is non-identifiable could be reduced, but only by adopting unrealistic assumptions. The problem lies with the identifiable expenditure which is 19 per cent above the UK average per head. If someone could find something wrong with these figures, they would be doing a great service, whatever the constitutional arrangements, but they are the most robust figures in the whole of the fiscal balance sheet.

The key to this problem lies in the definition and assessment of need. If expenditure is related to need, that is the only basis on which it can be defended in the longer term; and Scotland's needs, for the reasons outlined, do justify a higher level of expenditure per head than in England. But in the absence of a fresh needs assessment one cannot know how far the present gap between English and Scottish levels of expenditure can be justified. A needs assessment is liable to be contentious and it may bring results that would be unpalatable. Results would therefore only be acceptable if it was carried out not by a UK Government Department but by an independent body of the highest standing. It should cover not just Scotland but the other constituent countries of the UK and the English regions as well. Many of them also have substantial imbalances resulting in inter-regional fiscal transfers.

Once the true position is established, a strategy would have to be devised for bringing expenditure into line with justified need at a pace that can be tolerated. The difficulties are considerable. But that is surely better than allowing a situation to continue that can only produce raucous discontent between the countries of the UK and may eventually result in pressure to equalise far beyond what a needs assessment might indicate.

10

The economy, business and devolution

by Jeremy Peat and Stephen Boyle

Economic issues were at the heart of the devolution debate. Proponents argued it would bring economic benefits; opponents that it would damage the economy in Scotland and impair business.

Hopes of economic gains were high on the list of pro-devolution arguments from the outset. In 1973, the Kilbrandon Commission on the Constitution noted that "support for devolution... appears to be associated with an assumption... that it would bring an improvement in the material welfare of the people."[1]

And in the devolution White Paper *Scotland's Parliament* in 1997, the then Secretary of State wrote that: "With its new responsibilities, the Scottish Parliament will be in a position to encourage vigorous sustainable growth in the Scottish economy."[2] The pro-devolution consensus was clear: constitutional change would be an unalloyed 'good thing' for the economy.

But opponents were equally firm in their view that Scotland's economic prospects would be damaged. The big concern was the threat of higher taxes. Ian Lang, then Secretary of State for Scotland, summed up the argument thus: "the consequences of higher taxation would be dramatically bad. Inward investment would dry up overnight. The consequences of constitutional uncertainty would dry up investment. Companies would move south. Americans and Japanese and other foreign countries would cease to choose Scotland as their preferred location."[3]

1. Royal Commission on the Constitution 1969-1973, Report, Cmnd 5460, paragraph 372, October 1973.
2. Scotland's Parliament, Cmmd 3658 Foreword, July 1997.
3. Quoted in *The Herald*, 14 January 1995

A touch more pithily, his Cabinet colleague Kenneth Clarke, then Chancellor of the Exchequer, argued that if Scotland's Parliament had the "crazy power" to vary taxes, "Japanese inward investors will find Newcastle-upon-Tyne more attractive than Glasgow."[4]

So where does the truth lie? What could be the economic effects? How might traditional views about the role of economic policy change under devolution? And how is the new Parliament likely to affect the business environment?

The economy and the Parliament

Devolution will have economic consequences because the Parliament has economic powers. Its decisions could affect the overall level of activity in Scotland. It could, through a shift in the distribution of activity between, for example, the public and private sectors or the rich and the poor, affect living standards.

Predicting the net economic impact of devolution is neither simple nor straightforward. And much depends on events in the UK and in the world economy. The first step towards understanding the likely impacts is to establish how changes could arise. The second is to assess how the fact of devolution might itself bring changes in confidence and behaviour. Finally, we need to consider the impact of decisions taken beyond Scotland's borders in response to devolution.

Devolved powers

Some economic powers have been devolved to the Scottish Parliament while the UK government retains others. Table 1 summarises the key devolved and reserved economic policy matters.

The major levers of macro-economic policy have been retained at the UK level. Responsibility for taxation and the level of public spending remains at Westminster. Interest rate setting remains with the Bank of England.

4. Quoted in *The Herald*, 20 February 1996.

Who does what

Table 1 – Summary of key devolved and retained economic powers
Devolved
Local taxes to fund local authority expenditure
Education
Vocational training
Inward investment attraction
Support to indigenous firms
Infrastructure provision, mainly roads & local transport
Export promotion
Tourism development
Retained
Fiscal, economic & monetary policy
Relations with the EU
International trade
Currency
Competition law
Consumer protection
Designation of Assisted Areas
Social security
Employment law
Health & safety
Job search & support
Regulation of more than 15 industries

Source: Based on Scotland Act, 1998, Schedule 5

Devolving additional macro-economic powers would have enhanced the scope of the Parliament's influence and its ability to meet specifically Scottish needs. However, it enjoys control over many aspects of micro-economic policy.

Scotland's devolved government will find itself in a position similar to small nations within European Economic and Monetary Union (EMU). It will have limited influence over interest and exchange rates and very limited fiscal autonomy. But, like the small EMU states, it can pursue a distinctive micro-economic agenda. Those powers are sufficient to enable the Parliament and its Executive 'to make a difference' to Scotland's economic fortunes, because they can be used to boost the sustainable growth rate of the economy if that is the objective.

Policy tools at the Parliament's disposal include education and training, support for businesses – including inward investors – export promotion, tourism development and the provision of roads, local transport schemes and other infrastructure. But micro-economic measures such as these only affect the economy's capacity to grow at the margin and then mainly over the long term. Parliament may introduce appropriate measures and have the good judgement (or good luck) to do so in a favourable macro-economic climate. But it cannot deliver substantial economic benefits in a short time.

There is another reason why any benefits are likely to be limited. The Parliament faces significant constraints in the exercise of many of its powers. Even where it has significant micro-economic powers, such as financial assistance to businesses, trade promotion and the attraction of inward investment, Scotland's scope for wholly independent action is limited either in law or in practice by the UK Parliament, the European Union and the World Trade Organisation (WTO). Examples here include the UK's continuing control over the Assisted Areas map, EU rules on state subsidies to businesses, and emerging WTO rules on attracting inward investment.

Second, changing the micro-economic policy mix in Scotland in pursuit of economic benefits will have resource implications. New policies need not be more costly than existing ones. But the Parliament's ability to implement new policies depends upon resources being found for those purposes, even where net costs of securing a given objective remain the same as or lower than in the past.

There are several ways this could be achieved: efficiency gains in existing programmes, ceasing some existing activities, obtaining more money from Westminster or increasing revenue by exercising the tax varying power. Each may be feasible, but none represents an 'easy option', especially since Scotland's favourable public spending treatment extends to industrial assistance, as Chart 1 shows. As Gavin McCrone argues in Chapter 9, the resource noose is more likely to tighten than to slacken. The likely result is that policy will shift in an evolutionary way over a number of years, rather than in a radical manner from the start.

In *Scotland's Parliament, Scotland's Right*, the Scottish Constitutional Convention expressed the view that a devolved Parliament would enjoy influence over certain aspects of economic policy and that "these powers and

Regional aid shares

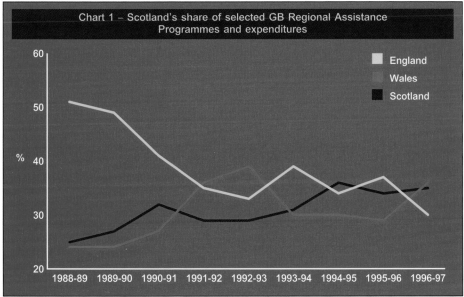

Source: Regional Trends 33, 1998 Edition, Table 13.9, page 159, Government Statistical Service

obligations will create a powerful psychology of economic responsibility". [5]

In arguing that the outcome would be a "Scottish economic renaissance," the Convention seemed to say that devolution could boost business and consumer confidence and might have a favourable impact on economic performance. New constitutional arrangements could affect sentiment and economic consequences could flow because people and firms changed their behaviour. Indeed, in the aftermath of the devolution referenda in Scotland and Wales, precisely this kind of point was made. One of the regular surveys of consumer confidence recorded levels of optimism in Scotland and Wales higher than in the rest of the UK. The accompanying report argued that "it seems likely that the prospects of devolution helped to further boost confidence in these areas". [6]

Yet this 'animal spirits' argument is unconvincing. It assumes, first, that under the previous constitutional arrangements people were – either in fact, or in their own perceptions – constrained in their actions and that under devolution they would be freed. Second, it assumes that the powers of the Parliament are sufficient to make people believe that economic conditions and opportunities would justify greater confidence and thus encourage them to behave differently. It is not evident that either condition holds. It is likely to take more than the fact of devolution and a new Parliament to bring about a sustained change in business and household confidence and behaviour.

The power to influence

The Parliament can exert influence even where it does not have legislative competence. Three examples illustrate the extent and limitations of this power. On the plus side, it is clear that, while

5. Scotland's Parliament, Scotland's Right, Scottish Constitutional Convention, 1995, quoted in Scotland's Parliament – Fundamentals for a New Scotland Act, The Constitution Unit, 1996, p. 134.
6. Consumer Market Quarterly Bulletin, Business Strategies Limited, January 1998, p. 20.

relations with the EU will continue formally to be a reserved matter, the Parliament and Executive will be able to exert a distinctly Scottish influence over economic – and other – policy matters in Europe which affect Scotland. Among the issues likely to be of immediate interest to Scotland are agriculture and fisheries.

A second area is the scope for potential influence. The Bank of England is charged by the Treasury with ensuring that in setting interest rates the Monetary Policy Committee (MPC) has 'proper' regional information. At present this is achieved through briefings given to the MPC by the Bank's Regional Agents. It is clear from the minutes of the MPC's meetings that regional issues feature in the Committee's deliberations. This means there is a pre-existing locus for the consideration of macro-economic conditions in Scotland – and other parts of the UK – and what these mean for monetary policy.

Thus, although macro-economic policy is a reserved power, the Parliament will have an interest in and, no doubt, wish to express a view on UK monetary policy as it affects Scotland. It has been argued that interest rates set for the UK as a whole have been inappropriate to Scotland's circumstances – always 'too high', never 'too low'. The Parliament could express such views to the MPC if it chose, though it would still be for the MPC to decide the extent to which UK conditions and its wider obligations allow it to accept such arguments.

Probably the most significant economic policy matter for Scotland to be determined during the Parliament's first term is whether the UK enters EMU. Under the existing constitutional arrangements this is a retained matter, not one for a devolved Scotland. However, the Parliament and Executive will be in a position to influence both Scottish public opinion and the wider UK argument. It lies with the Parliament and the Executive to set the tone and content of the debate in Scotland and to provide leadership. The way in which Scotland's government approaches the task will not only influence the debate. It will be an early test of the ability of the Parliament and Executive to lead the debate towards a conclusion consonant with Scotland's economic interests.

The extent to which the Parliament and Executive are able to exert influence over others depends, in part, on the strength of their arguments and the analysis that underpins them. We return in Chapter 11 to the important gaps in Scotland's knowledge about central aspects of its own economy. It is sufficient to note here that, while it is possible that the Parliament and Executive could exercise influence where they do not have formal powers, the effectiveness of their arguments and the probability of success will be increased if gaps in data and analysis are closed.

External influences

Devolution might lead to economic impacts by a final route. One consequence of constitutional change is that Scotland's relatively favourable treatment in terms of public expenditure per capita is the subject of increasing scrutiny in other parts of the UK, especially England.

At best, this awareness of Scotland's higher level of expenditure will mean a stricter application of the Barnett formula and erosion of Scotland's advantage in the years ahead. At worst, a further disenchantment in England over the scale of Scotland's advantage may lead to more rapid and substantial cuts in the resources available to the Parliament. This is more likely if Scotland is perceived to be profligate with public spending or if it pursues policies that conflict with the interests of the rest of the UK.

In the short term, any squeeze on the Parliament's resources would have negative implications for the Scottish economy. Public spending would fall and with it output and employment. The Parliament's ability to implement its programme would also be impaired.

A new role for economic policy?

One of the earliest benefits of devolution was unintended: the flowering of think tanks, policy institutes, seminar groups and conferences in what had previously been an unpromising terrain for new ideas. A notable feature of this work is the emphasis on the links between what have traditionally been thought of as independent policy measures and policy objectives. In particular, the scope for economic policy to serve a wider range of (non-economic) policy goals is now recognised.

For example, research could show how unemployment significantly influences a community's health record. If so, a range of 'economic policy' measures to bring people who have been unemployed for a long time back into the workforce could be deployed to support what are principally health objectives. Moreover, the answer to deep-rooted health problems in the area might have less to do with the amount spent on doctors and nurses or the number of hospital beds than conventional approaches suggest. Conversely, social, educational and public transport policy measures to tackle exclusion could be used in pursuit of explicitly economic objectives such as improving the quality of the labour supply.

The Parliament makes such innovative approaches to policy more feasible. But it will require new ways of managing resources and devising policy. It will also mean that public sector bodies, in particular, will have to be more innovative in how they work. 'Innovative' does not always mean 'good' or even 'better'. But it is encouraging that the Constitutional Steering Group (CSG) proposed that all Bills from the Executive be subject to an appraisal which considers fully all of their costs and benefits, not simply the financial ones.

Business and the Parliament

Just as the proponents of devolution may have exaggerated the timing and scale of any economic benefits, so too the opponents may have over-played the damage which might be done to business. With the exception of a few clearly defined areas, the Parliament has very little scope to affect the factors that are important in determining the business environment. The reality is that the Parliament's influence on Scottish business in its first term will be minor compared with issues such as the Millennium Bug, the restructuring of the EU's regional and agricultural aid funds and possible entry to EMU.

It is important to consider how the Parliament could affect the business environment given the powers at its disposal. But equally relevant here is the opportunity for business to influence legislators.

The business environment comprises the laws, regulations and customs that determine what people and businesses engaged in economic activities can and cannot do. These include rules on health and safety, insider dealing and corruption, the planning regime, tax laws and local authority rates, laws regarding minimum wages and maximum working hours, the regime of subsidy and support payments to business and so on.

Marxists (remember them?) would probably have said that they are the 'base' on which the 'superstructure' of capitalism is constructed. It is only by influencing the components of this 'base' that the Parliament will be able significantly to affect that environment.

Powers of the Parliament

It is clear that almost all of the most important means by which government can affect the business environment are not devolved to Edinburgh but retained elsewhere. Some examples emphasise the importance of the retained powers.

First, the Scottish Parliament cannot alter corporation tax rates, investment allowances, VAT or National Insurance contributions. Thus, it has no influence over any of the major direct fiscal policy determinants of the post-tax return on equity and, as Chart 2 shows, the extent of its influence over the total tax take is limited.

Second, health and safety laws stop employers from risking the lives and limbs of employees for higher profits. Some would argue that there is scope for extending and tightening existing legislation, for example to cover offshore oil and gas production. There is nothing in the powers of the Parliament that would enable this to happen, as health and safety is a retained power and matters concerning the Continental Shelf lie outside the Parliament's competence.

Finally, competition law determines what types of business practices are acceptable. It provides a framework for consideration of mergers and acquisitions, and governs relations between companies and between companies and customers. Competition law is, and will remain, a matter for the Westminster Parliament and, increasingly, the EU.

On the key levers of monetary and fiscal policy and on the main determinants of the business environment, the Parliament cannot change directly the operating environment for companies.

However, Parliament could affect the operating environment in two specific instances: by varying the basic rate of income tax and changing local government taxes. On income tax, the concern is not so much the general macro-economic impacts – research suggests these are likely to be modest – but the specific impact on the life and pensions industry. If there is scope for a different standard rate of income tax for Scottish residents, it follows that there should be a different rate of tax relief on pension contributions.

Scotland's tax pie

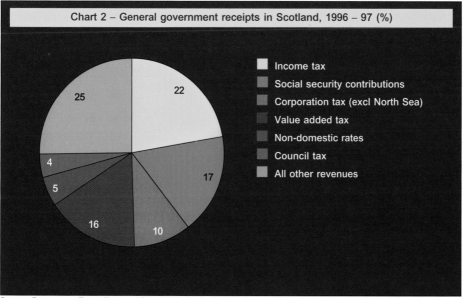

Chart 2 – General government receipts in Scotland, 1996 – 97 (%)

Income tax
Social security contributions
Corporation tax (excl North Sea)
Value added tax
Non-domestic rates
Council tax
All other revenues

Source: Government Expenditure and Revenue in Scotland, Table 9, page 22, Scottish Office Industry and Education Department, November 1998

This could involve pensions firms in considerable costs if parallel systems have to be introduced for Scottish and non-Scottish policyholders.

The power to vary local government taxation is potentially more significant. There are two local taxes. The council tax is levied on individuals and Non Domestic Rates (NDR) on businesses and other organisations. At present, a Uniform Business Rate (UBR) applies throughout Britain. It was introduced because widely varying charges were levied on similar businesses across the country. The variation in business rates often reflected the fact that some local authorities treated business ratepayers as a cash cow. Businesses do not have a vote, so there is a temptation to tax them rather than voters directly. It lies within the Parliament's powers to set the level of local authority taxes, to end the UBR or to devolve power over NDR to local authorities. The Parliament has limited revenue-raising powers. It is likely that local authorities will, from time to time, face resource constraints. It is quite possible, therefore, that there will be pressure to use business taxation as a source of additional resources for public spending programmes. In broad terms, an increase in NDR of less than 10 per cent would yield as much as increasing the basic rate of income tax by one percentage point. It would certainly be damaging to the business environment if UBR were abolished. In this respect the Parliament does have the power to affect that environment, for good or ill.

Influencing the Parliament

The CSG was set up after the 1997 referendum to help devise the Parliament's rules. Those who laboured in the CSG's field were determined that Holyrood would be a distinctly different animal from Westminster. One result is that the voice of Scottish business in Scotland's Parliament could be stronger and more effective than was the case at Westminster. The same opportunity exists for other groups because of some of the specific ways in which the Parliament works.

These stem from a commitment to openness and accessibility and to ensuring a participative approach to the development, consideration and scrutiny of policy and legislation. This gives rise to specific divergences from the Westminster model. First, before a Bill reaches the floor of the Parliament there will have been a pre-legislative, policy development phase involving, among other things, consultation with relevant interested bodies outside the Parliament. This process gives the opportunity to do more than comment on a Bill, which has already been drafted. It means that consultees will have the chance to affect the content of legislation. Put simply, if business thinks that a piece of legislation may affect it, there will be ample scope to influence the Bill at an early stage in proceedings.

Second, those who shaped the Parliament were keen to ensure that its members did not assume they enjoyed a monopoly on wisdom. So the Parliament's committees have the ability to establish expert panels of outsiders who can share with Members of the Scottish Parliament (MSPs) their knowledge and experience. Committees can also co-opt non-MSPs as non-voting members in order to utilise their expertise. Again, these changes afford the business community a considerable opportunity to make its voice heard and to ensure that business issues and expertise receive appropriate weight in the Parliament's deliberations.

In these ways the Parliament marks a clear departure from the past. It does so in a way which, far from threatening business, presents it with the chance to participate in the formulation of legislation and to ensure that MSPs are well informed about business issues. It is a long way from the manifest fears of devolution felt by many in the business community during the long years of debate.

Rising to the challenge

With hindsight, both sides made exaggerated claims about the effects of devolution on the economy and business. This chapter has sought to arrive at a more dispassionate judgement on these matters.

Devolution is not a panacea for Scotland's economic ills, and to expect rapid and substantial benefits is unreasonable. However, it is possible that the Scottish Parliament will adopt the kind of micro-economic policies which will boost the country's capacity to grow. This means breaking down the barriers to greater efficiency and productivity growth and exercising restraint in adding to business regulation. In its micro-economic powers, the Parliament enjoys considerable discretion.

If the possible economic benefits were overstated, so too were the threats to business. The scope of the Parliament's powers is too narrow to allow it to present any significant threat to business interests. There are some legitimate concerns about UBR, but on the other main determinants of the business environment devolution presents very few threats of substance.

Hindsight also suggests that the argument needs to move on. Devolution presents choices and real challenges for government and business. Recognising that it has powers, which can be used to stimulate the Scottish economy's capacity to grow, government's first job is to specify its own set of objectives.

Will it use its powers to that end, of more rapid and sustainable growth? Will it tackle the long-term tasks of improving the quality of the workforce and providing the circumstances in which indigenous enterprise can flourish? These are true challenges facing Scotland's Parliament.

11

What we don't know – and why it matters

by Jeremy Peat and Stephen Boyle

The problem

How well or badly off are the Scots? And is the economy in Scotland performing better or worse than the rest of the UK? The public requires authoritative and timely answers to these basic questions.

But how informed, and how timely, are the answers at present? In Chapter 2, Gross Domestic Product per head (GDP per capita) was used to compare the performance of the Scottish economy with its peers. While it is the best measure we have for making that kind of assessment, it does not give a very accurate picture of how affluent Scots are in comparison with people elsewhere.

The reason is that GDP measures the income created in Scotland but not the income that flows to Scottish households. This distinction matters. With high levels of inward investment, not all income created here will be retained in Scotland. A Japanese electronics company or a Canadian whisky distiller will send most of the profits from its Scottish operation to shareholders outside Scotland.

Similarly, Scots who own shares in non-Scottish firms receive income generated in other countries. To get a true indication of our affluence, the measure we really need is Gross National Product (GNP) per capita. That tells us how much income flows to Scottish households, after allowing for money flowing in from our investments outside Scotland and the amounts which go to non-Scottish shareholders from businesses located here.

If the Scottish Parliament wishes to see higher incomes in Scotland, it would be wise to track GNP per capita as a measure of progress towards the target. This is fine in principle but impossible in practice because we simply do not know the value of Scottish GNP. This is a simple statistic Standard Grade students learn to calculate at the age of 13 or 14, but a fact about the Scottish economy we do not know.

If that was all we didn't know about the Scottish economy, we could probably live with it. Unfortunately, other significant gaps render our knowledge of the economy in Scotland imprecise for policy-making.

Why the figures matter

Here we identify some of the more significant gaps and explain why they matter. We do not list all the gaps, or present a 'wish list'. However, we present some examples to illustrate how the Parliament's policy-making and influencing roles may be impeded by the paucity of data.

The availability of robust and timely data on various aspects of the economy is a necessary condition for sound policy-making. Policy cannot be made unless the economic backdrop is well understood. And information is needed to help a problem, to appraise the policy options open to government and to monitor and evaluate the implementation of measures.

Information and analysis are not ends in themselves. For politicians and policy makers, data and analysis are a means to an end. The ultimate end is improved living standards and that requires policies that are better formulated and delivered. So decisions about what information should be collected, from whom and with what frequency have to balance the prospective benefits against the costs. Benefits are often difficult to measure, but better information and analysis allow problems to be understood more accurately and solutions to be tailored to circumstances. The costs include not only the direct financial cost to government of collecting the numbers but also those costs to the providers – businesses and individuals – of supplying them.

Thus, when we argue for more data on aspects of the Scottish economy, it is because we believe it is necessary to support better analysis and the case is pressed with an acute awareness of the cost-benefit equation.

Priorities

Resources limit the amount of information which can be collected, so clear priorities are needed about where action is required. The guiding principle should be that data and analysis should support policy development and implementation. In Chapter 10 we described how the Parliament might make a difference to the Scottish economy and identified two principal ways: influencing other institutions and adopting new and different policies.

Scotland's inflation and growth rate

The Parliament will seek to influence a range of external bodies including the UK government and the European Union (EU). One of the main targets for influence will be the Monetary Policy Committee (MPC) of the Bank of England. Each month the MPC sets short-term UK interest rates. Only by chance will its decisions be equally suitable to all regions, because of different industrial structures and household behaviours. If there are concerns that Scottish circumstances differ materially from the rest of the UK and that interest rates are particularly important given that difference, evidence will be needed to support the argument.

The MPC considers all the factors which affect the inflation outlook for the UK, including how consumers are behaving, what's happening to the housing market, trends in earnings growth, the pattern of retail sales and movements in savings. It would be helpful indeed to know how each of these indicators was performing in Scotland but that is not possible. At The Royal Bank of Scotland, we have tried to plug some of these gaps, working with Scottish Homes and the Registers of Scotland to analyse the housing market and with the University of Edinburgh and the Scottish Retail Consortium to illuminate the retail scene. But gaps remain.

Beyond the determinants of inflation, it would be helpful to know Scotland's inflation rate. At present we have no idea whether prices here are rising faster or slower than in RUK.

The MPC often looks at the 'output gap' – the difference between the economy's capacity to grow and the speed at which it is growing. Knowing Scotland's current rate of growth measured by changes in GDP would, therefore, be particularly important. Under the present arrangements, however, the annual value of Scotland's GDP is published on a provisional basis around 11 months after the end of the relevant calendar year. The only quarterly output data for Scotland are for the 'production industries' – manufacturing, construction and energy – and are published on a provisional basis with a lag of about nine months. While the surveys produced by the Scottish Chambers of Commerce and CBI Scotland are helpful in hinting at what might happen, there is a major gap in official data about the service industries.

At the UK level, 'flash' estimates of GDP are available quarterly, with little delay and disaggregated between manufacturing, services and the other main sectors. Unless these basic facts are known, it is difficult to have an informed and credible discussion about output trends and inflationary pressures in Scotland and whether UK interest rate policy is appropriate to Scottish circumstances.

Lobbying in Europe

EU funds are important to Scotland's economy and especially to certain sectors and regions. The expansion of the Union's membership to include some poorer countries will put pressure on its budget. Some of the money Scotland receives will be under threat. As we pointed out in Chapter 10, one of the ways Scotland's Parliament could make a difference is by putting Scotland's case directly to Brussels.

In the case of the structural funds, the EU's regional aid programme, decisions about who gets what are often based on levels of income per head in an area. Scotland's negotiators could be handicapped in making their case because we do not have reliable and up to date information about income per head across the country.

Environmental policy

Both Conservative and Labour UK governments have emphasised the role of fiscal measures in achieving environmental goals. Staple features are the real terms increase in fuel duty and higher taxes on vehicles with large engines. There is also a growing lobby in support of road pricing. Just as interest rate changes may have an undue and disproportionate effect on regions, so too environmental measures of these kinds can have a disproportionate impact on Scotland.

In Scotland there has been a strong and consistent lobby that opposes them. But to date the debate has lacked comprehensive data. If the Scottish Parliament wishes to see this policy modified, it would need to put a more persuasive case to the Treasury than the self-evident observations that Scotland is further from the Channel than England, and that its population is distributed more sparsely. If the Parliament wants to influence that debate, it needs much more information about travel patterns, costs of travel and the environmental impacts of different measures in order to assess the effects of the alternatives on Scotland and other parts of the UK.

Informing micro-economic policy

Chapter 10 set out the Parliament's main micro-economic powers. They cover areas such as education, training, business support – including inward investment – infrastructure provision and trade promotion. The Parliament will also have responsibility for social housing, land use planning and many environmental matters, factors that affect economic performance. How might the Parliament's task be frustrated by the absence of robust data in these areas?

Education and training

One of the most important determinants of Scotland's long-term prosperity will be the extent to which its people have the skills and abilities needed to raise their productivity and maintain it at world-best levels. In Chapter 7 we questioned Scotland's recent performance in education and training. Those concerns arise from a study of data of varying quality from a range of sources. What is needed is a more reliable series of measures of Scottish education and training performance which can be compared where possible with Scotland's international peer group.

Significant steps have been made in recent years with the publication of school league tables and teaching and research assessments in universities. But when it comes to measuring the attainments of the working population, we are forced back on survey data which at the level of sectors and occupations in Scotland are too often inadequate for analytical and policy-making purposes.

If the data were available, it would be easier to identify priorities and differentiate between competing claims for resources. So, if budgets are constrained, what do the priorities of our economy and people most demand: more spending on pre-school, primary, secondary or tertiary education? Within tertiary education, what should be the balance of resources between higher and further education? In the field of vocational education and training, how should the Scottish Enterprise and Highlands and Islands Enterprise networks' decisions about the types of training to support be made? How can they justify these decisions to disappointed parties?

Supporting exporters

Government in Scotland has long devoted resource to export promotion and this is likely to be a focus of continued political interest. To ensure the support programmes give good value for money it is important to set targets and monitor performance against them. How much more should be exported by the assisted businesses, of what goods and services, by how many more firms and to which countries? Neil Hood reviewed the available data on Scottish trade in Chapter 3. However, for policy-making purposes these numbers may not by themselves be enough.

The main source is the Scottish Council Development and Industry's (SCDI) annual survey of exporters. The SCDI is to be commended on its magnificent efforts over the years to place decent export data in the public domain. Yet gaps remain. Energy and agriculture are outside the scope of the surveys and the recently added service sector survey will improve with time. Moreover, the data are not presented according to international standards that focus on commodities and not industries. Finally, the results appear after a lag of more than one year while the UK data are published on a monthly basis with little delay.

The other source is the Input-Output Tables – timeless fishing grounds for professional economists but not readily accessible or comprehensible to the interested lay person. While they identify Scottish exports to RUK, they do not detail the destination of overseas exports or the origins of non-UK imports.

For economic development policy purposes, there is another important issue regarding trade data. As Chapter 3 showed, manufacturing exports are dominated by the electronics industry. However, the measure used is effectively the gross value of sales. What we cannot easily tell is the value added content of Scottish exports. That is especially important in electronics, where so much of the value of sales is imported. If Scotland's Parliament wants to boost exports, presumably its focus will be net exports rather than just a gross figure that subsumes a significant amount of imports.

What is required is information on the volume and value of Scottish exports and imports by commodity, destination and origin.

Tourism

Peter Wood has highlighted the importance of tourism to Scotland's economy in Chapter 8. He made the point that tourism is not an industry in the conventional sense but a form of household activity which impacts on several industries. That means much of the conventional economic information that is available for Scotland –

employment, GDP, characteristics of the unemployed – gives almost no insight to tourism.

The Scottish Tourist Board's research team has sought to shed light on many aspects of the industry. At The Royal Bank of Scotland we have worked with them to produce the Scottish Tourism Index twice a year. Yet almost all of the information available comes from surveys. While these are conducted by extremely reputable companies and analysed by skilled researchers, surveys are always subject to sampling error. Thus, indicators of the number of visitors to Scotland, their origins, how much they spend, how they travel, when they come and go and where they stay are all essentially sample-based estimates.

There is widespread political agreement that tourism is important to Scotland's economy and government has continually intervened with support to the sector. Yet there is little concrete information available from which to judge the industry's performance or for government to decide about where its support should be targeted. More robust and timely information about who are Scotland's tourists, how they get here, where they go, when they arrive and what they spend would assist those tasks.

Access to publicly-funded research

One of the reasons we decided to write this book was to enhance knowledge about the Scottish economy, to inform debate about the kinds of issues that concern the Parliament. Improving the data flow would certainly enable more and better analysis of the economy. But there is another, very low-cost and short-term measure which the Executive and Parliament could take to raise the level of debate.

Government in Scotland and its various agencies has for many years commissioned a substantial volume of research work from commercial consulting firms and academics. The nature of this work ranges from audits of local and regional economies to analyses of sectors; from appraisals of policy options to the evaluation of measures. Between us we have commissioned and undertaken several hundred of these assignments over a number of years and we know the volume of material is substantial. Some of this can be commercially sensitive and probity demands that it remains confidential. However, much of it is not contentious.

This research is commissioned by public servants and paid for by taxpayers. Yet much of it remains distant from the public gaze when it could inform debate about just those aspects of micro-economic policy which could make a beneficial difference to Scotland's long-term prospects. The Constitutional Steering Group's desire that there is an extensive and fruitful pre-legislative debate before the Parliament passes laws is more likely to be a reality if such information is easily accessible.

It is perhaps no coincidence given the openness of Scottish Homes in publishing much of the research that it commissions, that there has been such an open discussion about housing policy in Scotland and that the terms of the debate have moved on so much in recent years.

Raising the quality of analysis

Allowing better access to existing research would be helpful. A regular flow of high quality research from academics and policy institutes would be more welcome still. Some of our academics undertake this kind of work now but their numbers are too few. One reason is that the type of research that supports policy-making does not always help universities and academics in the research assessment exercises that determine how much money they receive. There is an incentive to focus research on other topics.

We believe that the Scottish Higher Education Funding Council should alter the incentive structure to promote high quality, policy-relevant research on the Scottish economy. There is also a strong argument for a well-directed economic policy research institute with an appropriate balance of public and private funding. This could draw on the undoubted talents of the academic community and inform the Parliament and public on matters critical to Scotland's economy.

Lifting the veil

As the Parliament embarks on its historic journey, it is in danger of developing economic policy shrouded in a veil of ignorance. For Members of the Scottish Parliament it is not a matter of a choice between say, more nurses and teachers and spending money on enhancing data provision. Better information enhances analysis. That, in turn, should enable the Parliament to achieve and deliver on what it was established to provide: better choices for Scotland.

It is time to lift the veil.

Glossary

GDP	Gross Domestic Product
RUK	Rest of the UK, including Northern Ireland
RGB	Rest of Great Britain – i.e. England and Wales
nes	not elsewhere specified
nec	not elsewhere classified
EFTA	Europe Free Trade Association
FTE	Full time equivalent
MNE	Multinational enterprise
ATM	Automated Teller Machine
GVA	Gross Value Added
FTSE 100	Index of share prices of 100 largest companies, by market capitalisation, quoted on the London Stock Exchange and published by FTSE International Ltd
FTSE 250	Index of share prices of 250 largest companies, by market capitalisation, quoted on the London Stock Exchange and published by FTSE International Ltd
UKCS	UK Continental Shelf
ONS	Office for National Statistics
OECD	Organisation for Economic Cooperation and Development
NOMIS	Supplier of labour market and other data
WTO	World Trade Organisation
Total final demand	the total purchases of home produced and imported goods and services for private and public consumption, investment and export
DETR	Department of Environment, Transport and the Regions